Edited by:
Fr. Michael Sullivan
Archdiocese of New York

Contributions to Saints Biographies
Julie Cragon
Nashville, Tenn.

William J. Hirten Co.
35 Industrial Rd.
Cumberland, RI

Illustrated Lives of the Saints

St. Agatha

Saint Agatha was born in Sicily, the beautiful daughter of wealthy parents. At an early age, she consecrated herself to God. Agatha lived during the time when Christians were persecuted for their faith. Because of her beauty and her wealth, she was pursued by the governor of Sicily, Quintianus.

She rejected his proposals and he had her arrested, charged as a Christian and sent go live in a house of prostitution where he hoped she would be forced to change her life.

She prayed and wept and remained faithful to God despite the humiliation she suffered and the assaults she endured. Agatha miraculously maintained her virginity and after a month, Quintianus had her thrown in prison where she continued to profess her Christian faith.

To torture her, he had her stretched and burned with torches and finally had her breasts cut off. Thrown back in prison to die, Agatha was comforted by a vision of St. Peter who healed all of her wounds.

After four days, she was taken back to Quintianus who was not the least bit impressed by her miraculous cures. He ordered her to be rolled over hot coals and glass and returned to prison.

With this final prayer, "Lord, my Creator, You have always protected me from the cradle; You have taken me from the love of the world and given me patience to suffer. Receive my soul", Agatha died.

Feast Day: February 5
Name Meaning: Good, Virtuous
Patron Saint of: Bell ringers, breast cancer, bakers, against fire, nurses, wet nurses, martyrs.

St. Agnes

Saint Agnes was but twelve years old when she was led to the altar of Minerva at Rome and commanded to obey the persecuting laws of Diocletian by offering incense.

In the midst of the idolatrous rites she raised her hands to Christ, her spouse, and made the sign of the life-giving cross. She did not shrink when she was bound hand and foot, though the chains slipped from her young hands, and the heathens who stood around were moved to tears. The bonds were not needed for her, and she hastened gladly to the place of her torture.

Next, when the judge saw that pain had no affect on her, he inflicted an insult worse than death; her clothes were stripped off, and she had to stand in the street before a pagan crowd; yet even this did not daunt her. "Christ," she said, "will guard His own."

So it was. Christ showed, by a miracle, the value which He sets upon the custody of the eyes.

While the crowd turned their eyes away from the spouse of Christ, as she stood exposed to view in the street, there was one young man who dared to gaze at the innocent child with immodest eyes. A flash of light struck him blind, and his companions took him away half dead with pain and terror. Lastly, her fidelity to Christ was proven by flattery and offers of marriage. But she answered, "Christ is my Spouse: He chose me first, and His I will be." At length the sentence of death was passed. For a moment she stood erect in prayer, and then bowed her neck to the sword.

With one stroke her head was severed from her body, and the angels carried her soul to Paradise.

Feast Day: January 21
Name Meaning: Lamb, pure one
Patron Saint of: Chastity, Young Girls, Girl Scouts, Engaged Couples, Rape Victims.

St. Aloysius Gonzaga

A loysius was born in Castiglione, Italy in 1591. His father was military and expected his sons to train in military exercises and join in court life. When he was 8, Aloysius and his brother were sent to study and to serve in the court of Francesco de'Medici. At twelve, a kidney disease kept Aloysius in his room where he took the time to pray and to read about the lives of the saints.

He returned to Castiglione and met Cardinal Charles Borromeo, who gave him his First Holy Communion. He read books about the Jesuits and longed to become a missionary. He practiced by teaching catechism, fasting and rising in the night to pray. In 1581, his family moved to Spain where Aloysius and Ridolfo became pages in the court of Philip II. He remained pure despite the temptations surrounding him, keeping his eyes down and never looking at women. He had decided to join a religious order. His mother agreed but his father was outraged.

They returned to Italy where several members of his family tried to persuade Aloysius to forget about the priesthood but in 1585, he gave up all rights to his inheritance, went to Rome and joined the Jesuits.

Aloysius had a difficult time accepting the new rules set by the Jesuits. He was made to eat more and exercise with the other students and pray only during certain times of the day. When a plaque broke out in Rome in 1591, the Jesuits opened a hospital and Aloysius volunteered to work there. It wasn't long before he caught the disease and although he recovered, his health was never the same. He told his confessor, Robert Bellarmine of a vision he'd had showing that he would die in the Octave of the feast of Corpus Christi. On that day, he seemed well but requested the sacraments of the sick and the prayers of the dying which Cardinal Bellarmine administered. Aloysius died June 21, 1591, just before midnight.

He was canonized in 1726 by Pope Benedict XIII.

Feast Day: June 21
Patron Saint of: Young students.

St. Alphonsus Marie Liguori

Alphonsus Mary Anthony was born in 1696 in Marianella near Naples Italy. One of seven children, he was the son of a Neapolitan Nobleman and a devout Catholic.

He attended the University of Naples at sixteen and began practicing law by the age of nineteen. Despite his success as a lawyer and against his father's will, Alphonsus left his practice to become a priest.

He was ordained on 1726 and began work with the homeless youth in Naples, opening "Evening Chapels" as centers of prayer, community and education.

Several years later he went to live at the "Chiflese College" where he began training missionaries.

During a retreat at the college, Alphonsus met Sister Mary Celeste who told him of a vision she had that he was the one chosen to start the Congregation of the Most Holy Redeemer. The order was dedicated to preach and teach in the slums of the cities, to the most abandoned souls. In 1762 Alphonsus was appointed Bishop of Sant' Agata dei Goti. During this time he taught theology and wrote, tended to the poor and instructed those in need, reorganized the seminary and other religious institutions. Rheumatism deformed his body and he struggled physically. He died in 1787 and was canonized in 1839 by Pope Gregory XVI.

He was proclaimed a Doctor of the Church by Pope Pius IX. His works, "The Glories of Mary", "The Practice of the Love of Jesus Christ", and "The Visits to the Most Holy Sacrament", have had a great impact through the years.

Feast Day: August 1
Name Meaning: Noble and ready
Patron Saint of: Confessors, theologians, moralists.

St. Ambrose

Ambrose was born in Trier around the year 339. After his father died, he moved to Rome with his mother and later moved to Milan with his brother. He studied and practiced law and was appointed governor of Liguria and Aemilia, living in Milan.

The Arians and the Catholics were in a constant state of chaos and upon the need of appointing a new Bishop, tension arose and Ambrose was called on for help. As he addressed the people, someone yelled, "Ambrose for Bishop."

The crowd, both sides, began to chant for Ambrose who had not even been baptized but was still a catechumen. Within a week, Ambrose was baptized, consecrated Bishop of Milan and began formal instruction. He studied Scripture and the Early Church Fathers.

Ambrose gave all his money to the poor and all his land to the Church. He opened his door and allowed himself to be available to anyone in need of confession or guidance or leadership.

He fasted regularly, prayed continually, offered Mass daily and preached discourses that would later give him the title of Doctor of the Church.

Ambrose was called on time after time by different Emperors to help in political struggles. By 385, he had defeated Arianism in Milan and stopped the use of Churches as havens for the Arians. Ambrose also counseled the Emperor Theodosius after his massacre of thousands of men, women and children and subjected him to a public penance where he grieved for his mistake.

Ambrose was the first to address Church-state relations and to stress the supremacy of the Church in regards to morality and the Church herself.

Ambrose died on Good Friday, April 4, 397.

Feast Day: December 7
Patron Saint of: Bishops, learning, candle makers.

St. Andrew the Apostle

Saint Andrew was one of the fishermen of Bethsaida, and brother, perhaps elder brother, of St. Peter, and became a disciple of St. John the Baptist. He seemed always eager to make announcements. When called by Christ on the banks of the Jordan, his first thought was to go in search of his brother, and said, "We have found the Messiah," and he brought him to Jesus.

It was he again who, when Christ wished to feed the five thousand in the desert, pointed out the little boy with the five loaves and fishes.

St. Andrew went forth with his mission to plant the Faith in Scythia and Greece, and at the end of his years of toil to win a martyr's crown.

After suffering a cruel scourging at Patrae in Achaia, he was left, bound by cords, to die upon a cross.

When St. Andrew first caught sight of the cross on which he was to die, he greeted the precious wood with joy. "O good cross!" he cried, "made beautiful by the limbs of Christ, so long desired, now so happily found! Receive me into Your arms and present me to my Master, that He who redeemed me through You may now accept me from You."

For two days the martyr remained hanging on this cross alive, preaching with outstretched arms from this chair of truth, to all who came near, and asking them not to hinder his suffering.

Feast Day: November 30
Name Meaning: The Strong, Manly One
Patron Saint of: Fisherman, Sailors, Against Gout, Neck Problems.

St. Anne

Saint Anne was the spouse of St. Joachim, and was chosen by God to be the mother of Mary, His own blessed Mother on earth.

They were both of the royal house of David, and their lives were wholly occupied in prayer and good works. One thing only was missing from their marriage – they were childless, and this was held as a bitter misfortune among the Jews. After a long wait, when Anne was an older woman, Mary was born, the fruit of grace than of nature, and the child more of God than of man.

With the birth of Mary the aged Anne began a new life: she watched her every movement with reverent tenderness, and felt herself sanctified by the presence of her immaculate child.

But she had promised her daughter to God, to God Mary had consecrated herself again, and to Him Anne and Joachim led her up the Temple steps, saw her pass by herself into the inner sanctuary, and then saw her no more. Thus was Anne left childless in her lone old age, and deprived of her purest earthly joy just when she needed it most.

She humbly adored the Divine Will, and began again to watch and pray, until God called her to unending rest with the Father and the Spouse of Mary in the home of Mary's Child.

Feast Day: July 26
Name Meaning: The God Graced One
Patron Saint of: Grandmothers, Mothers, Housewives, House Keepers, Woman in Labor.

St. Anthony Abbott

Anthony was born in 251 in Egypt. His parents died when Anthony was about 20 years old and left with him a wealthy landowner with only one sister in his care.

After attending Church one day and hearing the Gospel message of Matthew, "If you seek perfection, go, sell your possessions, and give to the poor," Anthony sold all he had, put his sister in a convent and went outside the village to live like a hermit.

He wore animal skins, ate bread and water and prayed constantly.

With people coming to him for prayer and advice and healing, Anthony decided to move to the tombs farther from the village. He fought with the devil on several occasions and once, when the local villagers came to bring him food, they found him physically beaten and left for dead. They cared for him and when he recovered, Anthony moved farther out into the desert. He lived in a type of cell for twenty years, taking food and giving advice through only a small crack. Finally, a group of villagers went and broke down the door, worried about his physical well-being but found him in amazing health. Many around him were healed and those who stayed with him formed one of the first monasteries, living separately as hermits except to hear Anthony speak. Again, more people came for advice and healing, pulling him from his life of extreme prayer and service to God.

He left and went to a desert oasis where he spent the rest of his life praying, fasting and weaving mats. Although he left no formal monasteries, he was a great example of living an ascetic life. St. Anthony died in 356 at the age of 105.

Feast Day: January 17
Patron Saint of: Basket weavers, gravediggers, graveyards, hermits.

St. Anthony Mary Claret

Anthony Mary Claret was born at Salent in Catalonia, Spain in 1807. He trained to be a weaver, the trade of his father, and went to Barcelona to specialize. While there, he used his spare time for studying. He returned to Catalonia and entered the seminary at Vich in 1829. On the feast of St. Anthony of Padua in 1835, he was ordained and assigned to his home parish. Anthony traveled and preached and gave retreats. He founded a great religious library, the Libreria Claret, in Barcelona and wrote over 150 books.

In 1849, he founded the Missionary Sons of the Immaculate Heart of Mary, known as the Claretians.

At the request of Queen Isabella II, Anthony was made Archbishop of Santiago, Cuba. He reorganized seminaries, built hospitals and schools, validated thousands of marriages and gave local missions.

He traveled and the more he preached the greater the number of attempts on his life. After seven years, he was called back to Spain and became confessor to Queen Isabella II. He disapproved of the happenings in the Court but it allowed him to continue to preach, to write, to establish libraries and schools and to help revive the Catalan language. He took the opportunity to help in the appointments of bishops and other religious leaders in Spain.

In 1869, he left for Rome to participate in the First Vatican Council. His poor health forced him to retire to the Cistercian Abbey at Fontfroide in southern France. He died in 1870.

Feast Day: October 24
Name Meaning: Worthy of Praise
Patron Saint of: Weavers, Catholic Press, Claretians Missionary Sons of the IHM.

St. Anthony of Padua

In 1221 St. Francis held a general meeting at Assisi; when the others dispersed, there lingered behind, unknown and neglected, a poor Portuguese friar, resolved to ask for and to refuse nothing. Nine months later, "the eldest son of St. Francis," stood revealed in all his sanctity, learning, and eloquence before his astonished brethren.

Devoted from his earliest youth to prayer and study among the Canons Regular, Ferdinand de Bulloens, as his name was in the world, had been stirred, by the spirit and example of the first five Franciscan martyrs, to put on their habit and preach the Faith to the Moors in Africa. One night, when St. Anthony was staying with a friend in the city of Padua, his host saw brilliant rays streaming under the door of the Saint's room, and on looking through the key-hole he beheld a little Child of marvelous beauty standing upon a book which lay open upon the table, and clinging with both arms around Anthony's neck.

With an ineffable sweetness he watched the tender caresses of the Saint and his wondrous Visitor. At last the Child vanished, and St. Anthony, opening the door, ordered his friend by the love of Jesus whom he had seen, to "tell the vision to no man" as long as he was alive. Suddenly, in 1231, our Saint's brief apostolate was closed, and the voices of children were heard crying along the streets of Padua, "Our father, St. Anthony, is dead." The following year, in Rome one of its sons was inscribed among the Saints of God.

Feast Day: June 13
Name Meaning: to valuable to measure
Patron Saint of: Lost Articles, Oppressed People, Against Starvation, Amputees.

St. Apollonia

Apollonia was a virgin and martyr who lived in Alexandria during the persecution of Decius from 248 to 249.

She was a holy woman who spent her life taking care of others and performing acts of charity.

During the reign of Emperor Philip, Christians suffered cruel tortures at the hands of heathen mobs that pillaged homes and put many to death.

Apollonia was seized by a group of men who punched her repeatedly in the face, crushing all of her teeth.

The men then gathered sticks together in a pile outside the city and threatened to burn her at the stake if she did not deny her beliefs.

Like many of the Christians of the time, Apollonia suffered the decision to voluntarily take her life or denounce her faith or lose her virginity. Early Christian martyrs often had to choose an untimely death to hold fast to their beliefs.

As St. Augustine said, "Although they quitted life in this way, nevertheless they receive high honour as martyrs in the Catholic Church and their feasts are observed with great ceremony. This is a matter on which I dare not pass judgment lightly."

Before the men gathered around Apollonia so they could torture her further, she plunged herself into the fire and was burned to death as a symbol of her refusal to deny her faith.

Dionysius, the Bishop of Alexandria, knew all too well the sufferings of the Christians of the time and confirms in a letter to another Bishop the true strength of these people during the persecution.

Feast Day: February 9
Patron Saint of: Toothache, dentists.

St. Augustine

Saint Augustine was born in 354 at Thagaste, a provincial Roman city in North Africa. Although his mother, St. Monica, raised him in the faith, he left the church to follow the Manichaean religion. He went to Carthage and became a master in rhetoric and philosophy. Augustine took a mistress with whom he had a son, Adeodatus. In 383, he went to Italy to teach in Rome but instead moved to Milan where he met St. Ambrose. After reading an account of the life of St. Anthony of the Desert, Augustine underwent a profound conversion.

With the influence of St. Ambrose, the prayers of St. Monica and the friendship of St. Alipius, he converted to Christianity, quitting his teaching position and devoting his entire life to God.

Ambrose baptized Augustine and his son on Easter Vigil 387 in Milan. Upon the death of his mother, he returned to North Africa after spending time in Italy writing and praying. In 388, he sold all that he had and created a monastic foundation in Tapaste.

He was ordained a priest in Hippo Regius and his popularity spread as a famous preacher.

In 395 he was made coadjuter bishop of Hippo and occupied the see for 34 years. He was constantly writing and preaching against the heresies of the time. During the eighteen month siege of Hippo by the Vandals, Augustine spent much of his last days in prayer. He died in 430. He wrote many books including his Confessions and City of God.

He is a Doctor of the Church, a Western Father of the Church, and one of the most distinguished theologians in the history of the church.

Feast Day: August 28
Name Meaning: great; magnificent
Patron Saint of: Brewers, theologians, city of Carthage, printers.

St. Barbara

Saint Barbara was brought up a pagan. A tyrannical father, Dioscorus, had kept her jealously secluded in a lonely tower which he had built for the purpose of keeping her confined.

Here, in her forced solitude, she gave herself to prayer and study, and contrived to receive instruction and Baptism in secret from a Christian priest.

While in the tower she convinced some workmen who were building two windows to add a third in honor of the Trinity. Dioscorus, on discovering his daughter's conversion, was beside himself with rage.

He himself denounced her before the civil tribunal. Barbara was horribly tortured, and at last was beheaded, her own father, merciless to the last, acting as her executioner.

God, however, speedily punished her persecutors. While her soul was being carried by angels to Paradise, a flash of lightning struck Dioscorus, and he was rushed before the judgement seat of God.

Feast Day: December 4
Name Meaning: The Stranger or Foreigner
Patron Saint of: Miners, Architects, Builders, Brass workers, Stone workers, Artillerymen, Protection from lightning, Storms.

St. Benedict

Saint Benedict was born of a noble Italian family about the year 480.

As a young boy he was sent to Rome and placed in the public schools.

He was turned off by the lack of discipline and laziness of the Roman youth, so he fled to the desert mountains of Subiaco and lived as a hermit for three years in a deep cave. Legend has it that he was brought food by a raven flying to his cave.

He lived there unknown except by the monk Romanus who clothed him in a monastic habit.

His example of prayer and sanctity soon attracted others to join him.

The strictness of his rule also caused others to despise him and one even poisoned his drink but when Benedict made the sign of the cross on the bowl, it broke and fell into pieces on the ground.

After he built twelve monasteries in the mountains, he moved to Monte Cassino, where he founded an abbey and wrote his rule and lived there until he died. He had the ability to read consciences, prophesise and stop attacks of the devil.

He destroyed pagan temples and statues and drove demons out from pagan sacred sites.

At one point there were over 40,000 monasteries guided by the Benedictine rule which was basically "Pray and work."

Feast Day: July 11
Name Meaning: The blessed one
Patron Saint of: Against witchcraft, temptations, poisoning, dying people, monks, kidney disease, fever, civil engineers, school children.

St. Bernadette

ernadette Soubirous was born in a humble home in southern France on January 7, 1844. As a child, her health and her parent's poverty forced them to send her away to live with friends. But to prepare for First Holy Communion her mother insisted she return home. Soon after, while gathering wood near Lourdes, Bernadette first saw the vision of Our Lady in the grotto. Seventeen times again the frail little girl beheld the wonderful vision. She saw Our Lady for the last time on earth on July 16th, 1858.

Eight years later, while great numbers of pilgrims continued to visit the grotto, the Bishop eventually pronounced the visions authentic. Bernadette then entered the convent and became a sister of charity.

Her death in 1879 ended a life of illness and pain. Thirty years later, as Church authorities investigated her claim to sainthood, her body when exhumed was found perfectly preserved.

From the center of Christendom, St. Peter's in Rome, amidst majestic ceremonies of canonization, Pope Pius XI on December 8, 1933, the Feast of the Immaculate Conception, proclaimed her name to the world-Saint Bernadette.

Feast Day: April 16
Name Meaning: Brave as a Bear
Patron Saint of: Illness, poverty, Lourdes France.

St. Blaise

Saint Blaise lived in the fourth century and was the bishop of the city of Sebaste which is in the country of Armenia. He was also a physician who healed people and animals and according to legend, the sick animals would come to him for help but would never disturb him while he was praying. The church was being prosecuted in those days, so Blaise lived in a cave in the mountains.

One day a group of hunters seeking wild animals for the amphitheater came upon Blaise's cave.

They were first surprised and then frightened to see

the bishop kneeling in prayer surrounded by wolves, lions and bears. As the hunters dragged Blaise off to prison for being a Christian, a mother approached him with her young son, who had a fish bone stuck in his throat. At the Saints command the child was able to cough up the bone and was cured. The governor of Cappadocia tried to persuade Blaise to worship pagan idols. The first time he refused, he was beaten.

The next time he was hung from a tree and his flesh was torn with iron combs.

He was finally beheaded and became a martyr of the Church.

Feast Day: February 3
Name Meaning: The Stammerer
Patron Saint of: Healthy throats, builders, construction workers, veterinarians, animals.

St. Bonaventure

iovanni di Fidanza was born around 1221 at Bagnoregio in Tuscany. His name was changed to Bonaventure after he was healed from a serious sickness through the intercession of St. Francis who cried out, "O Buona ventura" which translates O good fortune! He entered the Franciscan Order and went to Paris to study.

He later taught scripture and theology at the Franciscan school in Paris until he was appointed Master General of the Franciscans in 1257. He worked hard to reorganize and reform his Order.

Although numbers increased, he still had a difficult time finding a middle ground between the rigorists who put poverty above everything and the moderates who wished the severities of the rule relaxed.

He was different from St. Francis in that he put great importance on study which required buildings and books. He viewed their mission as preaching and giving spiritual direction which directly complemented the work of the parish priests who were not prepared in that area. In 1273, Pope Gregory X appointed him Cardinal-Bishop of Albano.

When the messengers came with the news, Bonaventure had them wait outside until he finished washing the dishes. He was summoned to Rome to speak at the Council of Lyon in an attempt to help repair division between the Churches of the East and the West. He died July 15, 1274 before the council ended. He was canonized by the Franciscan Pope Sixtus IV in 1484. His multiple writings, valuable commentaries and lectures ranked him as one of the great Doctors of the Church.

Feast Day: July 15
Patron Saint of: Workers.

St. Brigid

Brigid was born around 452 in Ireland. Her father was a pagan chieftain and her mother his slave. Her mother was sent away and sold but after Brigid was old enough, she was returned to her father and put in charge of the dairy. Brigid was known for her generosity to the poor and the needy.

Stories are told of her giving away flour and milk and even her father's jeweled-encrusted sword.

Once old enough and freed from slavery, Brigid was sought after for marriage but she had vowed to enter the religious life.

It is said that she asked God to make her undesirable and her face became disfigured until she made her vows, at which time, her face recovered it's beauty. She and several other women were consecrated to the religious life by St. Mel, Bishop.

In the 470s, Brigid founded the Kildare Abbey, "church of the oaks," on the plains of Cil-Dara.

This small oratory developed into a Cathedral city, supporting a double monastery, one for men and one for women. From this monastery, a center for religion and learning, Irish missionaries were sent to preach and to teach; therefore, contributing to the spread of Christianity throughout the country. Brigid traveled extensively and founded many convents. She founded a school of art which specialized in metal work and illumination. Her scriptorium produced the Book of Kildare. Known for her wisdom and her generosity, stories of miracles surround the life of Brigid.

She died around 524.

Feast Day: February 1
Patron Saint of: Babies, blacksmiths, chicken farmers, children whose parents are not married, dairy workers, Ireland, midwives, poor, printers, scholars, travelers.

St. Camillus de Lellis

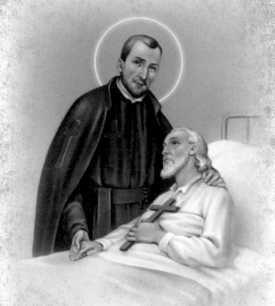

Saint Camillus was born at Bocchianico, Italy in 1550. His parents died when he was young and he joined the Venetian army and fought against the Turks. He was addicted to gambling and after losing all of his money, he worked construction on a building belonging to the Capuchins. There he was converted and became a novice but was unable to continue due to a diseased leg. He was cared for at St. Giacomo Hospital in Rome where he soon became part of the staff, caring for the incurably sick.

With the support of his confessor, St. Philip Neri, he left and established a congregation to care for the sick called The Ministers of the Sick or the Camillians. In 1584, Camillus was ordained a priest and with his congregation, enlarged their facilities and founded a new house in Naples. They made vows of poverty, chastity, obedience and perpetual physical and spiritual care of the sick. The men wore black robes with large red crosses on the chest and on the cape. They attended to plague victims on the ships in Rome's harbor and later to the troops in the first field medical units fighting in Hungary and Croatia.

In the face of the sick and dying, Camillus saw the person of Christ. In 1591, Pope Gregory approved the congregation known as the Camillians with Camillus as superior until he resigned in 1607. He died in Rome in 1619 and was canonized a saint in 1746 by Pope Leo XIII.

Feast Day: July 14
Name Meaning: Priest's assistant; temple servant
Patron Saint of: sick, nurses, nursing groups, hospitals.

St. Catherine of Alexandria

atherine was born in Egypt in the fourth century. According to popular tradition, Catherine was from a noble family and converted to Christianity following a vision. She was very intelligent, devoting herself to her studies and specializing in the sciences.

When the Emperor Maxentius began his persecution of Christians, Catherine, at the age of eighteen, presented herself before him and offered to debate his pagan philosophers. Amazed by her self-confidence, he agreed to the contest.

Catherine not only won the debate but also converted many of her adversaries by her arguments. They were put to death and she was beaten and put in prison. The Emperor's wife, anxious to meet this woman she had heard such great stories about, visited Catherine in prison. Along with one of the high officials and the soldiers of the guard, the Empress believed Catherine's teaching, and was converted and baptized. When Maxentius heard the news, he had them all put to death. Catherine was sentenced to be tortured on a spike wheel but upon her touch, the wheel miraculously broke apart. She was then beheaded.

Legend tells that Catherine's body was taken by angels to Mount Sinai where later a church and monastery were built in her honor. She is also said to have appeared to St. Joan of Arc and is listed as one of the Fourteen Holy Helpers.

Feast Day: November 25
Patron Saint of: philosophers, preachers, young maidens, female students.

St. Catherine Laboure

Saint Catherine Laboure was born on May 2, 1806 in the Cote d'Or, France. When she was nine, her mother died and she helped raise her younger siblings.

In 1830, she entered the community of the Daughters of Charity and while in the convent at the Rue du Bac in Paris, she received visions of Our Lady. The first vision occurred July 18 in the motherhouse. Catherine was awakened by a young boy dressed in white who told her, "The Blessed Virgin awaits you". Catherine followed him, assuming he was her guardian angel, to the chapel where she saw a lady seated at the right of the sanctuary. She walked up and knelt before her with her hands in her lap as the lady told her all about her life and how to act in difficult times and pointed to the altar as her source of consolation.

The lady predicted the anticlerical revolt in 1870 and told Catherine that she would give her a mission that would cause her suffering. Catherine was led back to her bed after she was instructed to tell only her confessor of the vision. On November 27, the Blessed Mother appeared giving her every detail of a medal she asked Catherine to have made and to promote.

It would become known as the Miraculous medal. Her spiritual director, Father Aladel, asked permission from Archbishop Quelen and the first fifteen hundred medals were made in 1832 and approved in 1836. Those who wore them told of the wonders that occurred through Mary's intercession while Catherine quietly cared for the sick at the Hospice d'Enghien.

A few days before her death she made known to others her visions of the Blessed Virgin. She died on December 31, 1876. She was canonized in 1947 by Pope Pius XII.

Feast Day: November 28
Patron Saint of: Pure, Virginal.

St. Catherine of Siena

Catherine, the daughter of a humble tradesman, was raised up to be the guide and guardian of the Church in one of the darkest periods of its history, the fourteenth century.

As a child, prayer was her delight. She would say the "Hail Mary" on each step when she was on the stairs, and was granted in reward a vision of Christ in glory. When she was only seven years old, she made a vow of virginity, and afterwards endured bitter persecution for refusing to marry. Our Lord gave her His Heart in exchange for her own, communicated with her with

His own hands and stamped on her body the print of His wounds. At the age of fifteen she entered the Third order of St. Dominic. From her obscure home she was summoned to defend the Church's cause.

Armed with Papal authority and accompanied by three clergy, she traveled through Italy, changing rebellious cities to be obedient to the Holy See and winning hardened souls to God. She found Gregory XI at Avignon and brought him back to Rome.

She was the counselor of Urban VI and corrected the disloyal cardinals who took part in electing an antipope. Long had she foretold the terrible schism which began when she died. Day and night she wept and prayed for unity and peace. But the devil turned the Roman people against the Pope, so that some sought his life. St. Catherine begged Our Lord to prevent this evil crime. The insurrection was subdued by Catherine's prayers but the devils showed their revenge by attacking the Saint herself, who gladly gave her life for God and His Church. She died at Rome at the age of thirty-three, A.D. 1380.

Feast Day: 29 April
Name Meaning: Pure One
Patron Saint of: Nurses, against fire, firefighters, illnesss, sexual temptation, miscarriages.

St. Cecilia

O n the evening of her wedding day, with the music of the marriage hymn ringing in her ears, Cecilia, a rich, beautiful, and noble Roman maiden, renewed the vow by which she had consecrated her virginity to God.

"Pure be my heart and undefiled my flesh; for I have a spouse you know not of; an angel of my Lord."

The heart of her young husband Valerian was moved by her words; he received Baptism, and within a few days he and his brother Tiburtius, who had been brought by him to a knowledge of the Faith, sealed their confession with their blood. Cecilia only remained. "Do you not know," was her answer to the threats of the prefect, "that I am the bride of my Lord Jesus Christ?" The death appointed for her was suffocation, and she remained a day and a night in a hot-air bath, heated seven times.

But "the flames had no power over her body, neither was a hair of her head singed." The lector sent to dispose of her struck with trembling hand the three blows which the law allowed, and left her still alive.

For two days and nights Cecilia lay with her head half severed on the pavement of her bath, fully sensible, and joyfully awaiting her crown; on the third day the agony was over, and in 177 A.D. the virgin Saint gave back her pure spirit to Christ.

She is the patron saint of musicians.

Feast Day: November 22
Name Meaning: The Blind One
Patron Saint of: Music, Musicians, Composers, Poets, Singers, Organ makers.

St. Charbel

Youssef Makhlouf, born in Northern Lebanon in 1828, was the son of a mule driver. He was three when his father died and he was sent to live with his uncle. Visiting his two hermit uncles in the monastery, he knew he wanted to some day be a hermit.

At age 23 he went to Our Lady of Maifouk monastery and after a year, joined the Maronite order at the Monastery of St. Maron. He took the name Charbel and two years later he professed his vows of poverty, chastity and obedience.

Charbel studied philosophy and theology at the Monastery of Kiffan and was sent back to St. Maron for his ordination in 1859. After 16 years Charbel was granted permission to live as a hermit on a hill near the monastery. He meditated all morning, celebrated Mass mid-day and prayed before the Tabernacle most of the afternoon and evening.

He was brought food from the monastery once a day. Charbel dedicated his life to the Eucharist. Through prayer and penance, he sacrificed his life so that others would return to God.

In 1898 Charbel suffered a stroke and died eight days later on Christmas Eve. Buried in the cemetery at St. Maron Monastery, dazzling lights were seen around his grave for 45 days after his death. When his body was exhumed, stories of healings spread. Charbel was canonized in 1977 by Pope Paul VI.

Feast Day: July 24.

St. Charles Borromeo

One of six children born to the powerful Medici family, St. Charles was recieved into the clergy at the age of 12. By age 22 he earned his doctorate in civil and canon law and was named cardinal-deacon by his uncle, Giovanni Angelo Medici, who had been elected pope the year before (Pius IV).

St. Charles acted as Secretary of State and papal legate in 1562, he convinced the pope to reconvene the Council of Trent and oversaw the writing of the catechism, missal and breviary called for by the council.

Although still only a deacon, St. Charles secretly received Holy Orders in 1563 and was consecrated Bishop a year later, taking the see of Trent which had been vacant for 80 years. St. Charles devoted the rest of his life to reforming the diocese, creating parishes and establishing monasteries. His radical reforms caused a lot of opposition at first, but his generosity and self sacrifice during the plague of 1576 made him beloved by his flock. He would sit by the roadside to teach the poor the Our Father and Hail Mary, and would enter the slums where the smell would force his attendants to choke. During the great plague, he refused to leave Milan, and was constantly by the sick and dying and even sold his own bed to help the poor. St. Charles died in Milan and was canonized a saint in 1610.

Feast Day: November 4
Name Meaning: The strong, manly one
Patron Saint of: Against ulcers, apple orchards, bishops, catechists, colic, catechumens, intestinal disorders.

St. Christopher

St. Christopher was a man of great strength but of a sensitive nature who wanted to serve the greatest King of the region.

But when he found the great King, he finds out that there is one who the King fears; the devil.

Then Christopher looked for Satan and served him until he found out even Satan stands in awe of someone; Jesus Christ. So Christopher searched long and hard for Jesus.

During the time he spent searching and learning about Christ, St. Christopher converted to the Catholic

Faith in Antioch, and was baptized by St. Babylas who told him he can best serve Christ by practicing the virtue of charity. St. Christopher then began carrying frail people and travelers across a raging stream.

One day he unknowingly carried the Christ Child across, and his burden became heavier at every step until it was almost unbearable, as Christ was carrying the weight of the sins of the world. To further prove His identity, Christ caused Christopher's staff to grow into a fruit-bearing tree.

This miracle converted many, and also angered the Emperor Decius, who had Christopher imprisoned, subjected to torments and beheaded.

Feast Day: July 25
Name Meaning: The Christ-Bearer
Patron Saint of: Travelers, Skiers, Truck Drivers, Bus Drivers, Water Peril, Violent Storms.

St. Clare Abbess

On Palm Sunday, March 17, 1212, the Bishop of Assisi left the altar to present a palm to a noble maiden, eighteen years of age, whom bashfulness had detained in her place. This maiden was St. Clare.

Already she had learned from St. Francis to dislike worldly comforts, and was secretly resolved to live for God alone. The same night she escaped, with one companion, to the Church of the Por-tiuncula, where she was met by St. Francis and his brethren. At the altar of Our Lady, St. Francis cut off her hair, clothed her in his habit of penance, a piece of sack-cloth, with his cord as a girdle. Thus was she espoused to Christ.

In a miserable house outside Assisi she founded her Order, and was joined by her sister, fourteen years of age, and afterwards by her mother and other noble ladies. They went barefoot, observed perpetual abstinence, constant silence, and perfect poverty.

While the Saracen army of Frederick II was ravaging the valley of Spoleto, a body of infidels advanced to assault St. Clare's convent, which stood outside Assisi.

The Saint had the Blessed Sacrament placed in a monstrance, above the gate of the monastery facing the enemy, and kneeling before it, prayed, "Deliver not to beasts, O Lord, the souls of those who confess to Thee." A voice from the Host replied, "My protection will never fail you." A sudden panic seized the infidels, who took to flight, and the Saint's convent was spared.

During her illness of twenty-eight years the Holy Eucharist was her only support and spinning linen for the altar the one work of her hands. She died A.D. 1253, as the Passion was being read, and Our Lady and the angels conducted her to glory.

Feast Day: August 11
Name Meaning: The Brilliant One
Patron Saint of: Embroiderers, Television, Against sores, Eyes, Goldsmith.

Sts. Cosmas and Damian

osmas and Damian were brothers, probably twins, born in the 3rd century in Arabia. Students of science, they both became doctors in the seaport of Aegea in Cilicia. They were known for treating each patient as brothers and sisters of Christ. They spent time healing spiritually as well as physically, teaching Christianity as they cured illnesses. Regardless of how much care a person needed, they never accepted a penny.

Cosmas and Damian were called anargyroi, which translated "the silverless".

Their charity caused them to be admired throughout the region. During the Diocletian persecution, they were arrested because of their Faith and brought to Lysias, the governor of Cilicia.

During extreme torture, they miraculously remained unharmed. There are stories of them being hung on a cross, shot with arrows, stoned and burned. Cosmas and Damian were finally beheaded along with their three brothers, Anthimus, Leontius and Euprepius around 287 AD.

Emperor Justinian I restored the city of Cyrus and dedicated it to Cosmas and Damian, but had their relics moved to Constantinople. Suffering from a serious illness, Justinian prayed for the intercession of the brothers and after he was healed, rebuilt and dedicated their church at Constantinople. At Rome, Pope Felix IV too built a church in their honor which is said to house the most valuable mosaics of the city. As well as other churches dedicated to the brothers, they are invoked in the Roman Canon of the Mass.

Feast Day: September 26
Name Meaning: sweet and harmless
Patron Saint of: Physicians, surgeons, pharmacists, dentists, barbers.

Sts. Cyril and Methodius

Cyril and Methodius were brothers born in Thessalonica in Greece in the early 800's. They joined a monastery until they were called out to be missionaries. They first worked with the Khazars, learned their language and converted many of their people. In the 860's, they were commissioned by Emperor Michael III to preach to the Moravians.

Cyril invented an alphabet and with the help of his brother, translated the Gospel and the necessary parts of the liturgy into the Slavic language.

German missionaries, already preaching in Moravia, were opposed to the use of the vernacular in the liturgy. The conflict caused the brothers to leave Moravia. Pope Nicholas I invited the brothers to Rome and his successor Pope Adrian II ordained a few of their disciples and approved the Slavonic liturgy. In 869, Cyril died and was buried in the Church of St. Clement. Methodius returned to Moravia and was later appointed Archbishop of Sirmium.

With more opposition from the German bishops, Methodius was exiled and imprisoned for two and a half years until the Pope sent for his release.

Constantly he had to defend his work and even after his death in 885, his successors continuously worked to use the Slavonic language in the liturgy. Before his death, Methodius had translated the entire Bible, with the exception of Maccabees, into Slavonic.

Feast Day: February 14
Patron Saint of: Bohemia, Bulgaria, Czechoslovakia, ecumenism, Moravia.

St. Dominic

Saint Dominic was born in Spain, A.D. 1170. As a student, he sold his books to feed the poor in a famine, and offered himself as ransom for a slave. At the age of twenty-five he became superior of the Canons Regular of Osma, and accompanied his Bishop to France. There his heart was nearly broken by the ravages of the Albigensian heresy, and his life was henceforth devoted to the conversion of heretics and the defense of the Faith.

For this reason he established his Dominican religious Order.

The convent for nuns was founded first, to rescue young girls from heresy and crime. Then a company of apostolic men gathered around him, and became the Order of Friar Preachers. Lastly came the Tertiaries, persons of both sexes living in the world.

God blessed the new Order, and France, Italy, Spain, and England welcomed the Preaching Friars.

It was in 1208, while St. Dominic knelt in the little chapel of Notre Dame de la Prouille, and implored the great Mother of God to save the Church, that Our Lady appeared to him, gave him the Rosary, and told him go forth and preach. Beads in hand, he revived the courage of the Catholic troops, led them to victory against overwhelming numbers, and finally crushed the heresy. His nights were spent in prayer; and, though pure as a virgin, three times before morning broke he did penance to himself.

His words rescued countless souls, and three times raised the dead to life. On August 6, 1221, at the age of fifty-one, he gave up his soul to God.

Feast Day: August 8
Name Meaning: The One Belonging to God
Patron Saint of: Astronomers, Astronomy.

St. Dominic Savio

Dominic Savio was born in Italy in 1842. By age five, he became an altar boy, attending Mass daily with his mother. Dominic was often found kneeling outside the church waiting for Mass to begin. He was allowed to receive his First Communion at age seven instead of the customary age twelve. Dominic knew the catechism and spent time preparing himself in prayer to receive the Eucharist. After meeting John Bosco on the Feast of the Rosary in 1854, Dominic was invited to attend school at the Oratory of St. Francis de Sales.

He organized a group called the Company of the Immaculate Heart to help John Bosco run the oratory.

He worked hard and followed the rules and was always filled with joy and cheerfulness. When Dominic attempted physical penances, John Bosco assured him that the best penances included obedience and humility and performing his daily work to perfection.

He began doing every small, simple task for the Glory of God.

Dominic once took the blame for a prank done to a priest by two of his classmates. When asked later why he stayed quiet about the false accusation, Dominic said he was trying to imitate Jesus who remained quiet when falsely accused. He helped solve arguments, assisted classmates in their spiritual life and encouraged frequent Confession and Communion.

In 1857, Dominic acquired tuberculosis and was sent home to his parents. He knew he was dying despite the doctor's reports and asked for the parish priest who heard his confession, gave him Communion and administered the Anointing of the Sick. Dominic died at the age of fifteen. He was canonized June 12, 1954 by Pope Pius XII.

Feast Day: May 6
Patron Saint of: Choirboys, falsely accused.

St. Dorothy

Saint Dorothy followed her parent's footsteps by being martyred for the Christian faith, most likely during the time of the Emperor Diocletian's persecution. St. Aldhelm relates that St. Dorothy was tortured at the hand of the governor in Caesarea due to her refusal to worship idols, as well as her refusal to marry. She believed that Christ was her only spouse. Two women who were sent to tempt Dorothy to renounce her faith were instead converted by her. A well known tradition relates that a lawyer named Theophilus taunted Dorothy on her way to her execution, which took place in the winter, telling her to send him some roses or apples "from the garden of her Spouse." Before Dorothy was executed, an angel in the form of a child appeared with a basket of roses with apples, and Dorothy sent the child with the basket to Theophilus. Upon receiving these gifts, he realized their divine origin and was converted to the Christian Faith. Eventually, he himself becoming a martyr for the Faith. In some countries fruit trees are blessed on her feast day because of her connection with a blooming fruitful miracle.

Feast Day: February 6
Name Meaning: A gift of God
Patron Saint of: Brewers, brides, florists, gardeners, midwives, newlyweds.

St. Dymphna

Saint Dymphna was born in the seventh century when Ireland was almost universally Catholic. Yet, her father, a chieftain, was a pagan.

He was a man of great wealth and power. Her mother was of noble descent and a devout Christian. Dymphna was a sweet and attractive girl. When she was fourteen her mother died and her father was afflicted with a mental illness brought on by his grief.

Her father sent messengers out to find a replacement for his wife to fill the void in his life.

Their search was fruitless. They then suggested, he marry Dymphna because of her resemblance to her mother. Under the stress of mental illness her father was suffering from, he was willing to follow this scandalous proposal. Dymphna was filled with disgust over the idea and dedicated herself to a life of virginity.

Dymphna, her priest and two friends decided to flee the country from her father. They went by boat and landed in Belgium where some hospitable villagers received them in their home. Her father was very angry at her disappearance and eventually tracked them down. He tried to persuade her to come back but her priest rebuked him for his wicked proposals. Her father then had the priest beheaded and again asked his daughter to return. She again refused him, thus infuriating him to the point that he then beheaded her. She was only fifteen years old when she died and was buried in a pure white tomb in a cave.

Feast Day: May 15
Name Meaning: Little fawn
Patron Saint of: Mental Illness, mental illness healthcare workers, martyrs, epilepsy, rape victims, incest victims, runaways.

St. Elias

lias, the Greek form of Elijah, was known as the Tishbite. He was a prophet whom God chose to bring the Israelite people back to the One True God. During the reign of Ahab, an altar to Baal was erected in the temple which Ahab built in Samaria. The Old Testament book of Kings says that Ahab did more to anger the Lord than any previous kings.

Thus, Elijah tells Ahab that the land will suffer a long drought. The Lord tells Elijah to move east of the Jordan.

The ravens bring him bread and meat in the morning and in the evening and he drinks from the river. As the water dried up due to the drought, the Lord sends him to a widow who takes care of him with her last bit of flour and oil and in return, she and her son were able to eat for a year without her flour or oil jar every going empty. After three years, Elijah returned to confront Ahab and asked him and the other followers of Baal to meet on Mount Carmel.

On the mountain they sacrificed two bulls and each prayed but only One True God answered with the fire for the sacrifice.

Despite Elijah's work, Jezebel, wife of Ahab, would not change and sent others to kill Elijah.

As he fled and hid, the Lord spoke to him and directed him further to anoint Hazael as king of Aram, Jehu as king of Israel and Elisha as prophet to succeed him. He met with Ahab again and prophesised the death of Jezebel and evil that would be on his family during the reign of his son. Following all that the Lord had requested, Elijah and Elisha stood together in front of the Jordan. Elijah parted the water with his mantle and shortly after was taken in a whirlwind up to heaven in a flaming chariot with flaming horses.

Feast Day: July 20
Name Meaning: the Lord is my God
Patron Saint of: Against earthquakes and draughts.

St. Elizabeth Ann Seton

Saint Elizabeth was born in New York City in 1774 and raised in a devout Episcopalian family. At the age of 19, she married William Magee Seton and they had five children.

She and her sister-in-law Rebecca became involved in social work and organized the Protestant Sisters of Charity to work among the poor in the city.

With a failing business and her husband's poor health due to tuberculosis, Will and Elizabeth sailed to Italy as an effort to save his life. She was left a widow at 29, in a strange country and without her children.

However, because of the strong faith of her new friends in Italy, Elizabeth was attracted to the Catholic faith. Upon her return to America, she joined the Catholic church which caused her to be rejected by many of her friends and family. She was invited by Bishop John Carroll to move her children to Baltimore and open a school next to St. Mary's Seminary.

It was the first Catholic free school in America.

She moved to Emmitsburg and opened a school for poor children. Despite the loss of her oldest daughter to tuberculosis in 1812, Elizabeth continued to persevere. She established community life with the first of her Daughters of Charity and in 1813, seventeen more women made their vows. In 1816, her youngest daughter, Rebecca, died and with her eyes fixed on the Blessed Sacrament, Elizabeth too died of tuberculosis in 1821.

The first miracle credited to her intercession was the cure of a nun with cancer in New Orleans, Louisiana. She was canonized in 1975 by Pope Paul VI.

Feast Day: January 4
Name Meaning: My God is an oath or My God is abundance
Patron Saint of: Death of children, in-law problems, loss of parents, opposition of Church authorities, people ridiculed for their piety, Diocese of Shreveport, Louisiana, widows.

St. Elizabeth of Hungary

Saint Elizabeth Queen of Hungary was only twenty-four when she died. Her father was the King and her aunt was St. Hedwig.

She was married at the age of thirteen to a young nobleman named Louis. Her mother in law tried to stop the marriage and mocked Elizabeth because of her charity and humility. She stated Elizabeth was unfit to be Queen because of the way she behaved by constantly prostrating before the crucifix. She humbled herself by wearing the simplest clothes woven of unthreaded wool and eating as little as possible.

She refused to wear her jeweled crown because Jesus wore one of thorns. More important than this was her constant and remarkable charity, which was expressed in every detail of her life.

When she was not working on the business of government she spent all her time either at prayer or visiting the poor and the sick to an extent that her husbands family accused her of squandering the royal treasure on the vagrants of the land. After her husband died, his family took control of power and ousted Elizabeth and her four children from the palace.

They forbid anyone to take her in, but finally she accepted help from her uncle the Bishop of Banberg.

Eventually her husbands friends returned from the Crusades, and they had the duty to protect Elizabeth.

They were prepared to fight for her but her husbands family stepped aside and Elizabeth regained her position as queen and her son as the rightful heir to the throne. She lived only a few years longer and spent them in constant prayer and charity.

She was canonized four years after her death by Pope Gregory IX.

Feast Day: November 17
Name Meaning: One consecrated to God
Patron Saint of: Homeless people, death of children, bakers, widows, those in exile, falsely accused, brides.

St. Expeditus

xpeditus was possibly a Roman centurion born in Armenia. Many stories surround this saint who upon declaring his Christianity was visited by the Devil in the form of a crow and told to wait until the following day for his conversion.

Expeditus stomped on the bird, killed it and declared, "I'll be Christian today!" He was beheaded during the Persecution of Diocletian in 303.

Expeditus is pictured holding a cross on which is written the word "hodie", meaning "today".

He is stepping on a crow which from his mouth streams a word ribbon with the text "cras", meaning "tomorrow". As another story explains, a group of nuns in Paris received a crate labeled "expedite" containing the relics of a saint. The nuns assumed that the relics belonged to St. Expeditus and prayed for his intercession for their needs.

When their prayers were answered quickly, devotion to the saint spread throughout France. Similarly, the chapel of Our Lady of Guadalupe in New Orleans received a shipment they had been expecting along with a crate marked "expedite" with the statue of a saint enclosed they assumed to be St. Expeditus.

He has since worked for the many rapid solutions requested by those who believe and he is associated with those who have to deliver things on time.

Feast Day: April 19
Name Meaning: quickly
Patron Saint of: expeditious solutions, against procrastination, merchants, navigators, emergencies.

St. Faustina

Helen Kowalska was born in 1905 in Glogowiec, Poland. She was the third of ten children born in a poor family who struggled during the years of World War I on their little farm. She attended school for three years and at the age of fifteen began working to help support her family. She believed she had the calling to be a nun and applied to many convents until she was finally accepted as a Sister of Our Lady of Mercy. She became a nun in 1926 and took the name Sister Maria Faustina of the Blessed Sacrament.

Not having much of an education, she usually worked as a gardener or a cook or a housekeeper.

On February 22, 1931, Jesus appeared to her bringing a message of Mercy. She tells that Jesus was dressed in white with His right hand raised in a blessing and the other touching the garment at the breast. Two large rays came forth from the garment, one red and one white or pale. She was told by Jesus to paint this image of Him and at the bottom put the words, "Jesus, I trust in You". He also asked that the First Sunday after Easter be celebrated as the Feast of Mercy. With the help of Fr. Michael Sopocko, devotion to the Divine Mercy spread.

Sister Maria Faustina kept a diary, later published as "Divine Mercy in My Soul: The Diary of St. Faustina". In 1935, she had a vision teaching her the Chaplet of Divine Mercy. Sister Faustina became sick in 1936 but continued to pray for the conversion of sinners and to recite the Chaplet of Divine Mercy.

She died in 1938 and was canonized the first female Polish saint by Pope John Paul II in 2000.

Although her published works were forbidden by the Vatican for twenty years, when Pope John Paul II was Archbishop of Krakow, Sister Faustina's life was reinvestigated and the devotion to the Divine Mercy was permitted and has now spread all over the world.

Feast Day: October 5
Patron Saint of: World Youth Day.

St. Fiacre

Fiacre was born in Ireland around the sixth or the seventh century. He lived in a hermitage in County Kilkenny and became known as a holy man.

People from all over would come to him for advice or healing. Looking for a more solitary life, he moved to Meaux, France and went to the Bishop, St. Faro, in search of a quiet dwelling place.

Faro gave him a piece of his own property in Breuil. Legend says that Faro offered him as much land as he could plow in a day.

Fiacre turned the earth with the point of his staff, plowing down trees and weeds without effort.

He built a cell for himself, a shelter for visitors and those in need, and an oratory in honor of the Blessed Mother. Daily he worked in the garden and led a life of prayer and fasting. His herbs were known to cure and once again people came from all around for his guidance and healing. He welcomed them all, feeding them and serving their needs. Even after his death around 670, miracles of healing at his tomb and near his shrine at Breuil were reported. He did not allow women to enter his hermitage or his chapel.

The story is told that when Fiacre miraculously turned the land he needed, a woman reported that she had seen him do witchcraft. Of course, Faro knew the truth and confirmed Fiacre's faithfulness to God.

St. Fiacre is known as the patron of gardeners as well as cab drivers because the French cabs are known as fiacres since the first horse and carriage for hire was near the hotel Saint-Fiacre.

Feast Day: September 1
Patron Saint of: Gardeners, cab drivers.

St. Florian

Saint Florian lived in the third century AD in the area of modern day Austria and Bavaria. He was the commander of the Roman Imperial Army. At that time in history the Church's followers were going through an intense persecution. The Emperors sent an edict to all the Roman provinces proclaiming that all followers of Christ be executed. The governor of where Florian was stationed was a vicious man named Aquilinus.

He began rounding up Christians in the noble town of Lauriacum and brought them before a judges tribunal where they would be tried and executed.

When Florian heard of this he gave all his personal wealth to the poor, gathered forty of his soldiers and left to Lauriacum. When he reached the town he publicly declared himself a Christian and refused to worship the pagan idols. He was then seized by the governors soldiers and savagely tortured.

Seeing that Florian could not be overcome by pain of the body he was sentenced to die. They tied a large mill stone around his neck and hurled him from a bridge into a river and was drowned in order to terrify his followers. St. Florians body was recovered by a pious woman and was given a proper burial.

In 1138 Pope Lucius III gave some of his relics to King Casimir of Poland and to the bishop of Cracow.

Since that time, St. Florian has been regarded as a patron of Poland. Many miracles of healing are attributed to his intercession and he is invoked as a powerful protector in times of danger from fire or water. It is said that Florian stopped a town from burning by throwing a single bucket of water on the blaze and thus became known as the patron saint of firefighters.

Feast Day: May 4
Name Meaning: The flower bud one
Patron Saint of: Against battles, against fire, barrel-makers, brewers, chimney sweeps, coopers, drowning, fire prevention, firefighters, floods, harvests.

St. Frances Xavier Cabrini

Saint Frances Xavier Cabrini was born July 15, 1850 in Lombardia, Italy the youngest of thirteen children. At age eighteen, she tried twice to enter the convent but was refused due to poor health. She helped her parents until their death and then worked the farm with her brothers and sisters. In 1874, Monsignor Serrati asked Frances to run the House of Providence Orphanage at Codogno but the original foundress opposed Frances and the institution was closed. At the request of the bishop of Todi, Frances and seven followers moved into an abandoned friary and founded the Missionary Sisters of the Sacred Heart to care for poor children in schools and hospitals. The congregation was approved in 1880 and expanded to Rome and Milan. Frances sought the advice of Pope Leo XIII to continue her work in China; however, he advised her to send missionaries to the United States. He told her "not to the East, but to the West". In 1889, she and six other sisters were invited by Archbishop Corrigan of New York to work with Italian immigrants. The archbishop was forced to withdraw his invitation due to lack of facilities but Frances stayed in America. She encountered many hardships but her reputation grew and local store owners donated whatever they could to help her in her work. She frequently had to return to Italy which meant she had to overcome her extreme fear of traveling over water. She also had difficulty learning the English language; however, because of her faith, her deep trust in God and her wonderful administrative abilities, she founded schools, hospitals, and orphanages to aid Italian immigrants and children. She founded religious houses and charitable organizations throughout the United States, Italy, England, France, Spain and South America. She became an American citizen in 1909 and died in Chicago on December 22, 1917. She was canonized in 1946 by Pope Pius XII. She was the first American citizen to be canonized a saint.

Feast Day: November 13
Name Meaning: Free
Patron Saint of: Immigrants, hospital administrators, orphans.

St. Francis of Assisi

rancis was born at Assisi in Umbria in 1181 or 1182. The son of a wealthy cloth merchant, he enjoyed an easy life. He was very well liked by everyone and considered a leader among his peers. Francis longed to be a knight so when Assisi and Perugia went to war, he joined the fight. Captured and imprisoned for a year, Francis was ransomed only to resume his old ways. He longed for glory but on the way to his next battle, dressed in fine armor, he had a dream in which God told him to return home to Assisi.

Francis turned to God in prayer and solitude to

discover his calling. Kneeling below the crucifix in San Damiano Church, he heard God tell him, "Francis, repair my church." Of course, Francis thought God meant the church where he was kneeling so he immediately went out and sold some of his father's fabric to get money for the repairs. Furious, his father demanded his money back. Francis returned the money, denounced his inheritance and stripped himself of the clothes on his back. Begging for stones, he rebuilt San Damiano and two other deserted Chapels, St. Peter's and St. Mary of the Angels. Francis took the Gospel message literally, gave away all he had, served the poor, took nothing for the journey and as others joined him, went out two by two to preach penance, brotherly love and peace. He and his followers went to Rome to have their order approved by Pope Innocent III. Francis was made a deacon so he could read the Gospels in Church.

A few years later, a young girl, Clare, heard him preach and together with her sister Agnes, joined Francis to form an order for women known today as the Poor Clares. Francis was known for his love of all of God's creation. As his order grew, he allowed others take over leadership and he retreated to the mountainside in solitude. There, amongst nature and in poverty, he received the stigmata, the five wounds of Christ. Two years later, in 1226, Francis died.

Feast Day: October 4
Name Meaning: Free
Patron Saint of: Animals, Ecology, Merchants, Environment.

St. Francis Xavier

aint Francis came from a wealthy family and studied at the University of Paris. There he met St. Ignatius of Loyola, whose rigorous spiritual lifestyle at first gave him second thoughts about entering into religious life. Eventually, however, at the age of 28, he entered St. Ignatius's new Society of Jesus and became one of the first seven Jesuits to take his vows.

Six years later, he was sent out as a missionary to India and Japan. He was ship wrecked three times, often spent days without food and was attacked by the

Muslims. He ministered to the sick and imprisoned, taught children and worked to correct the immoral life style which the Europeans who lived in that area of the world were engaged in.

He journeyed through India preaching and working miracles, and even raised the dead to life. Francis had always dreamed of evangelizing China, but became ill and died on an island off the coast of China.

St. Francis baptized hundreds of thousands of people, destroyed forty thousand idols in the pagan East, built over 100 churches and raised about 25 people from the dead; all in 10 years. There are now millions of Catholics in the Orient who can trace their Christian evangelization back to Francis Xavier. He is regarded as the greatest missionary since St. Paul.

His body is preserved incorrupt.

Feast Day: December 5
Name Meaning: The free man
Patron Saint of: African missions, foreign missions, navigators, parish missions, plague epidemics, propagation of the faith.

St. Gaetano

Gaetano was born at Vicenza in 1480. The son of the Count of Thiene, he studied civil and canon law at Padua University.

He worked as a prothonotary Apostolic in Rome under Pope Julius II. He was ordained in 1516 and returned to Vicenza due to the death of his mother.

He founded a hospital for incurables where clergy worked to heal the spiritual as well as the physical needs of their patients.

He realized the need to form a group combining monastic prayer and service to the poor.

Gaetano returned to Rome and began to lay the foundation for the new order. Giovanni Pietro Carafa, Bishop of Chieti (in Latin: Theate) and later Pope Paul IV, was elected first superior of the Theatines.

The focus was to live like the Apostles of old, preaching and teaching and caring for the needs of the poor and the sick. He worked to revive frequent participation in the sacraments and to recall the priests to spiritual discipline and scripture study. His order grew slowly.

During the sack of Rome in 1527, the Theatines escaped to Venice where they continued their work.

They established the order in Verona and in Naples. While in Naples, he founded a "pawn shop" or bank which helped the poor and later became the Bank of Naples. Despite all his good work, Gaetano became sick over the troubles of the Church and of his homeland. He refused a mattress and died lying on boards, imitating Jesus on the cross.

Feast Day: August 7
Patron Saint of: Job seekers, unemployed.

St. George

he devotion to this holy martyr dates back to at least the fifth century and, it can be proved that the oldest of the churches dedicated to his honor in Constantinople were built by Constantine the Great, which would be a much earlier date. Very little is known of his life.

It is supposed that he suffered martyrdom in the persecution under Diocletian at Nicomedia, in the beginning of the fourth century. Among the Greeks he is called the Great Martyr and his feast is kept as a holy day of obligation.

The intercession of the saint was implored especially in battles, as he is said to have been a soldier.

Under the first Norman kings, he was chosen as patron saint of England and Edward III instituted an order of knighthood in his honor.

There are some who suppose that it was St. George who tore down the imperial edicts of persecution when they were first published at Nicomedia.

He is generally represented as engaged in combat with a dragon, which has long been considered a symbol of evil as the devil is called a dragon in the book of the Apocalypse. The story is called the Golden Legend where a dragon who lived in a lake in Lybia, defeated whole armies by the fierceness of this creature.

The monster ate two sheep each day and when they were gone, young women were then substituted.

St. George heard the story on a day when a princess was to be eaten. He crossed himself, rode into battle on his horse against the serpent and killed it with a single blow of his spear. He then made a great sermon and converted all the local people. The reward he was given by the King was given to the poor and he rode away.

Feast Day: April 23
Name Meaning: The farmer
Patron Saint of: Boy scouts, field workers, lepers, skin diseases, soldiers, shepherds, syphilis, agricultural workers, farmers.

St. Gerard Majella

Saint Gerard is one of the most famous
miracle workers in the history of the
Catholic Church. During the process of
the cause for his canonization, many miracles revealed
were attributed to St. Gerard. From the day of his birth
on April 6, 1726, until his death at the age of twenty-
nine, Saint Gerard was an example of weak health.
That was why he was three times denied admission to
a religious order. And yet, after he was received into
the Redemptorist Order, even with his spare frame
and pallid face, it was found that he could do "the

work of four." After being admitted as a brother in the Order, he traveled the Italian countryside as a missionary and became the instrument thru which Christ's healing powers were channeled.

Even today through his intercession he continues to help the faithful who ask for his prayers. No one has been able to answer satisfactorily why Saint Gerard has come to be considered the patron of mothers.

On several occasions during his life, his prayer saved the life of a mother and her new-born child. And after his death, and before his canonization, several instances of this special patronage over mothers were recorded. But in the two centuries since his death, Saint Gerard's dominant virtue - trust in God's Providence - have brought more and more to seek his intercession.

His favorite expression, "God will provide" hurls a ringing contradiction at the timidity of a materialistic world. Over two hundred years ago, the saint once remarked: "If anyone unable to bear the sufferings which God has sent him; calls on me for help… or if I hear of such a one, I will pray that God give him the grace of conformity with His holy will." St. Gerard's feast day is celebrated on October 16th.

Feast Day: October 16
Name Meaning: The Spear Carrier
Patron Saint of: Pregnant Women, Mothers, Falsely Accused, Child Birth.

St. Hedwig

Hedwig was one of eight children born to the Duke of Croatia. She was born in 1174 in Andechs, Bavaria and at the age of twelve was married to Henry I of Silesia.

Hedwig had great influence in her husband's decision making.

Together they opened hospitals, founded religious houses, re-established monasteries and cared for the poor, the sick and the homeless. They had seven children and after the birth of the last child took a vow of celibacy before the Bishop of Breslau.

Hedwig prompted Henry to donate land and build the Convent of the Cistercian nuns at Treibniz which he founded in 1202.

This was the first house for religious women in Silesia and one of Henry and Hedwig's daughters, Gertrude , became the abbess. Hedwig moved near the Convent at Treibniz and often joined with them in their works of mercy.

Hedwig was well respected for her spiritual kindness and her holiness. The story is told of a war between Henry of Silesia and Conrad of Masovia over the possession of Cracow. Although Henry won the war, Conrad surprised him in a church and took him captive. Hedwig went to Henry's aide and her mere presence changed Conrad and he released Henry. She preached peace within her family and her country.

After the death of Henry in 1238, Hedwig entered the Cistercian Convent but did not take the vows so she could continue to distribute her wealth to the poor. She died in 1243.

Feast Day: October 16
Name Meaning: Refuge in Battle
Patron Saint of: Against jealousy, Bavaria, brides, death of children, difficult marriages, duchesses, Germany, Silesia, widows.

St. Helen

It is generally believed by the Church historians of England, that St. Helen was born in that country, and according to legend, was the daughter of Coel a British king who lived in friendship with the Romans. Constantius, at that time an officer in the Roman army in Britain, married her, and raised Constantine, their eldest son who received his education under Helen's eyes. In 293, Constantius joined the empire with the title of Caesar, obtaining the government of Gaul and Britain. St. Helen was not at that time a Christian, but after the accession of her son,

Constantine and his miraculous victory, she embraced the Christian faith and the most heroic practices of Christian virtue. Her dutiful son had her proclaimed empress and struck medals in her honor. In spite of this new dignity she helped the people at the divine offices, in plain clothes and used her wealth for charity to the poor and in the building of churches. When the emperor decided to erect a church on Mount Calvary, St. Helen, although eighty years old, wanted to oversee the work, and left for Jerusalem, hoping to find the Holy Cross. Excavations were made, and three crosses were discovered. A plaque which lay near one of the crosses and perhaps the nail marks by which it had been attached, seemed to indicate which was the cross of our Saviour. A miracle decided the question. A sick person, being touched by the three crosses was instantly cured at the touch of the cross which Christ had died on. St. Helen built two magnificent churches, one on Mount Calvary, the other on Mount Olivet. After travelling through the East, she beautified the city of Drepanum in honor of St. Lucian and Constantine afterwards gave it the name of Helenopolis. Her journey had been marked by great deeds of virtue and by many works of charity. She died at Rome in August, 328, or 326, in the twentieth year of her son's reign. Constantine made her hidden works to be known and erected a statue to her memory.

Feast Day: August 18
Name Meaning: The light
Patron Saint of: Difficult marriages, divorced people, converts, archeologists.

St. Hubert

Saint Hubert was born about 656, the eldest son of Bertrand, Duke of Aquitaine. As a youth, Hubert went to the court of Neustria, Paris where his charm and manners won him popularity with the dignity of "the court of the palace". He was warmly welcomed by Pepin Heristal, mayor of the palace, and quickly made grand master of the household. About 682, he married Floribanne, daughter of the Count of Louvain, who died giving birth to their son, Floribert. Hubert withdrew to the forest and put all his energy into hunting. On Good Friday morning, when everyone else was crowding into churches, Hubert went to the forest to hunt. The story is told that as he was chasing a huge stag, the animal turned and Hubert saw a large crucifix between its antlers. He heard a voice say, "Hubert, unless thou turnest to the Lord, and leadest a holy life, thou shall quickly go down into hell." Hubert protrated himself and said, "Lord, what wouldst Thou have me do?" The answer came, "Go and seek Lambert, and he will instruct you." St. Hubert was welcomed by Lambert, bishop of Maastricht who soon became his spiritual director. Hubert gave his birthright to the Aquitaine to his brother Odo and made him guardian of his infant son. He studied for the priesthood, was ordained, and became one of St. Lambert's chief associates in his diocese. Hubert made a pilgrimage to Rome in 708 and while he was gone, Lambert was assassinated by the followers of Pippin. Hubert was appointed the thirty-first bishop of Maastricht. In 720, in obedience to a vision, Hubert moved St. Lambert's remains from Maastricht to Liege of which Lambert is the patron and Hubert the first bishop. Hubert successfully worked in the forest of Ardennes to put an end to the worship of idols. Upon his visit to Fura during the dedication of a new church, Hubert became sick and died peacefully praying "Our Father, who art in Heaven…". He was buried in the church of St. Peter, Liege but his bones were later moved to the Benedictine Abbey of what is now known as St. Hubert, Belgium.

Feast Day: November 3

Name Meaning: Shining of Mind

Patron Saint of: Hunters, mathematicians, opticians and metalworkers.

St. Ignatius of Loyola

Saint Ignatius was born on December 24, 1491 at the castle of Loyola in Guipuzcoa, Spain. In 1506, he became a page in the service of a distinguished noble.

The following year , he joined the army and while defending the small town of Pamplona was severely injured by a cannonball. During his long recovery, Ignatius read numerous texts on the life of Christ and the lives of the saints.

Moved by their heroic deeds, he underwent a profound spiritual conversion. In 1522, he traveled to the Benedictine monastery of Montserrat where he left his sword on the altar of Mary in dedication to her.

Emulating Francis of Assisi, he then spent months in a cave near the town of Manresa and began his famed Spiritual Exercises. In 1523, he went to Rome and then to Jerusalem but returned to Barcelona to study.

He spent the next eleven years studying at Alcala, Salamanca, and Paris, and it was during this time that he met companions, including Francis Xavier, who would be the core of his group, known today as the Jesuits. They took vows of poverty and chastity, with the hope of doing missionary pilgrimages to the Holy Land but with the promise of special service to the Pope. In 1537, they traveled to Italy to be ordained.

Pope Paul III officially recognized their society, the Society of Jesus, in 1540. Ignatius was elected the first Superior General of the order and received the first solemn profession on April 22, 1541.

He wrote the Jesuit Constitutions and spent the rest of his life working for the Society, caring for the sick and the poor, and founding colleges and universities to educate the clergy as well as the laity. He founded the famous Gregorian College in Rome. From 1553 to 1555, Ignatius dictated his life story to his secretary which is a valuable key for understanding the Spiritual Exercises. He died in Rome on July 31, 1556.

Feast Day: July 31
Name Meaning: Son, Fire
Patron Saint of: Spiritual Exercises, Spain, Jesuits, soldiers, retreats.

St. James the Apostle

Among the twelve apostles, three were chosen as the familiar companions of our blessed Lord and of these James was one. He, alone with Peter and John, were admitted to the house of Jairus when the dead woman was raised to life.

They alone were taken up to the high mountain, and saw the face of Jesus shining as the sun, and His garments white as snow and these three alone witnessed His agony of Gethsemane.

It was James who demanded fire from heaven to consume the inhospitable Samaritans, and who sought the place of honor by Christ in His Kingdom.

When St. James was brought before King Herod Agrippa, his fearless confession of Jesus crucified so moved the public prosecutor that he declared himself a Christian on the spot. Accused and accuser were hurried off together to execution, and on the road the prosecutor begged for James' forgiveness.

The Apostle had long since forgiven him, but hesitated for a moment whether publicly to accept as a brother one still unbaptized. God quickly recalled to him the Church's faith, that the blood of martyrdom supplies for every sacrament, and, falling on his companion's neck, he embraced him, with the words, "Peace be with you!" Together then they knelt for the sword, and together received martyrdom.

His relics are in Compostela Spain where he is patron saint of pilgrims. The Spanish army would ride into battle with the cry "Santiago!" (Saint James)

Feast Day: July 25
Name Meaning: The supplanter
Patron Saint of: Against arthritis, arthritis suffers, pharmacists, veterinarians, laborers, pilgrims.

St. Jerome

Jerome was born at Stridon near Aquileia in the early 340's. He went to Rome where he studied rhetoric, grammar and the classics, along with Greek and Latin. He was baptized between 360 and 366, took some time to travel and then settled in Aquileia where he became a monk.

He traveled to Antioch around 374 where he became seriously ill.

While he was sick, he had a vision that convinced him to set aside his secular studies and devote his life to God.

He became a hermit in the Syrian Desert and for five years learned Hebrew so he could study the Scriptures in their original language.

He returned to Antioch and was ordained a priest by Bishop Paulinus. He went to Constantinople where he studied Scripture under St. Gregory Nazianzen and began to translate the early writings of the Church from Greek to Latin. He went back to Rome and worked with Pope Damasus I.

During this time, Jerome spent time on Biblical translations, wrote a number of commentaries on the Bible and began to produce a Latin text of the entire Bible called the Vulgate. He gave spiritual instruction to a group of wealthy widows but his angry disposition and sharp temper gave him a bad reputation.

He moved to Bethlehem in 385 along with his brother Paulinianus, some friends and eventually many of the women he instructed.

They supported him in his efforts to establish a monastery and several convents. He died in 420 in Bethlehem and was buried beneath the Church of the Nativity. His remains were later moved to St. Mary Major in Rome.

Feast Day: September 30
Patron Saint of: Scholars, Librarians.

St. Joan of Arc

The most illustrious heroine of all time, St. Joan of Arc, was born on January 6, 1412 of simple parents at Domremy in France. Taught by her mother from her earliest years to pray each night "O God, save France," she could not help but think that the great love for her country as a child would later consume her life.

While the English were overrunning the north of France, their future conqueror, unschooled in worldly wisdom, was peacefully tending her flock and learning the wisdom of God at a small shrine in the fields.

While hearing voices from heaven, she was approached by St. Michael, who appeared to her, so she could save her country from the enemy. She immediately hurried off to inform the King and convince him of her divine mission. Just as her banner, inscribed "Jesus, Mary," appeared on the battlefield she rushed to the forefront of the battle of Orleans. She then led Charles VII to be crowned at Rheims.

Later, abandoned by her King, she fell into the hands of the English, who gave her a mock trial and burned her as a heretic. But the Maid of Orleans had at last received her reward. With a greater celebration than any king had, while being crowned and amid the acclamations of the whole world, on May 13, 1920, Pope Benedict XV proclaimed her St. Joan of Arc.

Feast Day: May 30
Name Meaning: God is gracious
Patron Saint of: Martyrs, captives, prisoners, rape victims, France.

St. John Baptist de la Salle

Saint John Baptist de la Salle was born on April 30, 1651 in Reims, France. He was the oldest of ten children, born of a noble family, who dedicated himself to the religious life at age eleven. He was ordained a priest in 1678 and a few years later received a doctorate in theology.

Concerned for the education of the children of poor families, John helped open two schools where students could attend for free. Realizing the low quality of the teachers, he became involved in opening a house for the training of teachers. In 1683, he resigned as canon of the cathedral, gave away all his worldly possessions and dedicated himself to the training of young men in education. He and twelve others took vows and formed themselves into an order called the Brothers of the Christian Schools, also known as De La Salle Christian Brothers or simply the Christian Brothers.

He opened several more schools and training colleges for teachers. John changed the techniques of teaching by changing from one-on-one instruction to classroom teaching, adding religious education to teacher training and using the vernacular instead of Latin. John urged teachers to take time with their students and to treat them with love and concern for their spiritual growth.

His popularity spread across Europe and King James II asked him to come to England to teach the young boys in the royal court. He opened a college for Irish teachers in 1698. Although he was opposed by secular schoolmasters and critics of his techniques, he remained active and persevered until 1717.

He suffered from asthma and rheumatism in his later years and died in 1719 at Saint-yon. He was canonized in 1900 by Pope Pius XII.

Feast Day: April 7
Name Meaning: God is Gracious, Gift of God
Patron Saint of: Teachers, educators, school principal.

St. John the Baptist

The Birth of St. John was foretold by an angel of the Lord to his father, Zachary, who was offering incense in the Temple. It was the destiny of St. John to prepare the way of Christ. Even in the womb he knew the presence of Jesus and of Mary, and he leaped with joy at the glad coming of the Son of man. In his youth he remained hidden, because Jesus' life was hidden also.

But before Christ's public life began, a divine impulse led St. John into the desert where in silence and in prayer, he began to purify his own soul.

Then, as crowds broke in upon his solitude, he warned them to flee from the wrath to come, and gave them the baptism of penance, while they confessed their sins. At last there stood in the crowd One whom St. John did not know, until a voice from within told him that it was his Lord.

With the baptism of St. John, Christ began His penance for the sins of His people, and St. John saw the Holy Spirit descend in bodily form upon Him.

At that point the Saint's work was done. He had but to point his own disciples to the Lamb, he had but to decrease as Christ increased.

He saw all men leave him and go to follow Christ. "I told you," he said, "that I am not the Christ".

St. John was beheaded soon after by Herod and his wife Salome for boldly rebuking them for their scandalous life style of adultery. He died a martyr about one year before the crucifixion of Jesus.

Feast Day: June 24
Name Meaning: Gift of God
Patron Saint of: Baptism, Bird Dealers, Epilepsy, Convulsions.

St. John Bosco

Saint John Bosco was born in 1815 in Italy. His father died when he was two, leaving his mother to raise three boys. In his youth he worked as a shepherd and added any odd jobs he could find to help his family.

John was sent messages about God's will for his life through dreams. He knew through these dreams that God wanted him to work with young, underprivileged children. He attracted hundreds of young people to meet and to pray and to learn the catechism. To keep their attention, John juggled and performed magic tricks. He explained the homilies the priests gave and as word spread of his incredible stories, adults joined to listen to him. He wrote short explanations of the faith and taught the children how to print them.

He began studying for the priesthood and was ordained in 1841. He opened a boarding house with his mother, "Mamma Margaret", including workshops to teach trades such as shoemaking, printing, bookbinding, and iron working. As other priests came to help, the foundation was laid for the first Salesian Home. The importance of John's work spread and resulted in the building of technical schools and workshops. In 1868, he built a church dedicated to Our Lady, Help of Christians. Pope Pius IX approved the Society of St. Francis de Sales, the Salesians, followed by a similar order for women, the Daughters of Our Lady Help of Christians.

At the time of his death in 1888, there were nearly a thousand priests working in 250 houses of the Salesian Society all over the world.

Feast Day: January 31
Name Meaning: God is gracious; gift of God
Patron Saint of: Apprentices, boys, editors, laborers, students, young people.

St. John the Evangelist

Saint John, the youngest of the apostles in age, was called to follow Christ on the banks of the Jordan during the first days of Our Lord's ministry.

He was one of the privileged few present at the Transfiguration and the agony in the garden.

At the Last Supper his head rested on the side of Jesus, and in the hours of the Passion, when others fled or denied their Master, St. John kept his place by the side of Jesus, and in the end stood by the cross with Mary.

From the cross the dying Savior bequeathed His Mother to the care of the faithful apostle, who "from that hour took her to his own;" fittingly, as St. Austin says, "to a virgin was the Virgin entrusted."

After the Ascension, St. John lived first at Jerusalem, and then at Ephesus.

He was thrown by Domitian into a caldron of boiling oil, and is thus reckoned a martyr, though he was miraculously preserved from harm.

Afterwards he was banished to the isle of Patmos, where he received the heavenly visions described in the Apocalypse. He died at a great age, in peace, at Ephesus, in the year 100.

Feast Day: December 27
Name Meaning: God is gracious
Patron Saint of: Against Poison, Paper Makers, Art Dealers, Printers, Painters.

St. John of God

John Ciudad was born in Portugal in 1495. At the age of eight, he ran away to Spain with a visiting priest and was left to work as a shepherd with a family willing to care for him.

In 1522, he joined the Spanish army and a life of drinking and gambling. Fourteen years later he left the military and worked as a shepherd while contemplating his life. He searched for his parents only to find that they had died. Still unsettled, he decided to go to Africa to ransom Christians captured by the Moors.

On the ship he met a family that he served for a while but soon decided to move back to Spain.

He opened a religious bookshop and sold items for little profit to try to spread the faith.

Then, one day during a festival in the town, John heard Blessed John Avila speak. He was so filled with deep sorrow for his past that he gave away all his books and all he owned and ran around the city beating his chest and screaming, calling upon God's forgiveness. The people of the town thought he had gone crazy and had him committed to a mental hospital.

John of Avila told John to stop all the open repentance and begin finding positive ways to atone for his past sins. John of God began caring for the people in the hospital. Upon his release, he began working in the streets of Granada caring for the sick and the poor. At night, he sold firewood to help pay for food and supplies. He soon found a house for rent and opened a small hospital. He begged for money for beds and medicine. Priests and doctors donated their time and soon other men joined John in his ministry, forming the Brothers Hospitallers of St. John of God.

Stories spread of his unselfish devotion to the poor and the sick and the helpless. He died in 1550 after trying to save a person from drowning.

Feast Day: March 8
Patron Saint of: Booksellers, hospital workers, printers, sick.

St. John Neumann

John Neumann was born in Bohemia in 1811. He studied in Prague and hoped to be ordained in 1835 but due to an over-abundance of priests or his desire for missionary work, he had to leave his home to follow his vocation.

At age 25, after learning English by working in a factory with those who knew the language, he came to New York and was ordained at old St. Patrick's Cathedral. His parish stretched from Lake Ontario to Pennsylvania and he traveled from village to village visiting the sick and saying Mass wherever he found a table. He helped teach the German and the Irish children to read and write.

Longing for community life, he joined the Redemptorists and was the first to make vows in the United States. He preached to the immigrant communities in Ohio, Pennsylvania and Maryland.

In 1852, he was appointed Bishop of Philadelphia. He built churches and established the first diocesan Catholic school system. He founded the Sisters of St. Francis, a new congregation for women. He founded the first national parish for Italians in the United States and was the first to introduce Forty Hours Devotion in his diocese.

He cared for God's people where they needed him, when they needed him and in their own languages. He died in 1860 and was buried in St. Peter Church in Philadelphia. He was canonized in 1977.

Feast Day: January 5
Patron Saint of: Authors, Deaf.

Pope John Paul II

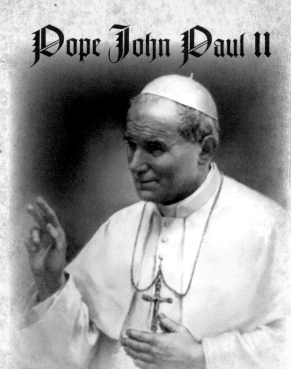

ope John Paul II was born Karol Joseph Wojtyla in Poland in 1920. His mother died when he was a young boy so he was raised by his father and his older brother. He loved sports as a youngster and was an excellent student at school. He also loved the theater and literature and wanted to be a professional actor.

During WWII and the Nazi occupation of Poland he worked as a stonecutter while belonging to an illegal Catholic organization and still acting in the theater secretly. He then decided on a vocation in the priesthood in 1942 and was ordained in 1946. After only twelve years of being a priest he was named auxilliary Bishop of Krakow and a full bishop four years later. He was a born leader, an attribute which was noticed by Pope Paul VI who elevated him to Cardinal in 1967. In 1978 at the age of 58, he was elected to the Papacy.

He was the first Polish Pope and also the first non-Italian Pope since 1522. John Paul II changed the way the Papacy was looked upon by the outside world. He traveled the world to bring the church's message to his flock by way of example as did the apostles. In 1981 he was shot by a Muslim assassin in St. Peters Square on the feast of our Lady of Fatima. He miraculously survived the wounds and attributes his survival to Our Lady's intervention.

He was a prolific writer who wrote many books on spirituality and countless encyclicals to move the church toward the true teaching of Christ. John Paul passed on in 2005 but will be forever remembered as one of the most dynamic and great Popes ever to succeed St. Peter.

St. John Vianney

Saint John Vianney was born in 1786 in France, the son of a shepherd. At age twenty, he began studying for the priesthood and after a short stay in the army, returned to study at Lyons seminary.

John was not a good student and because of his difficulty with Latin, had to be tutored.

His goodness and piety led to his ordination in 1815. Three years later he was made the parish priest of Ars, a small village. Known as the Cure of Ars, he spent his life preaching, hearing confessions and living his life constantly in pursuit of the heart of Jesus. He visited his parishioners, especially the sick and the poor. He fasted and prayed and spent many sleepless nights for the intentions of his people.

He often spent up to sixteen hours a day in the confessional, reminding people of sins they had forgotten and did not want to confess.

His reputation spread and crowds of people came to him from all over the world for spiritual advice and reconciliation. It was told that he multiplied loaves of bread for his orphanage, La Providence.

He was known for bringing thousands back to the Catholic church. Refusing all offers of promotions and honors, John remained at Ars his entire life.

His works of charity and love and conversion were known throughout the world. He died in 1859.

Feast Day: August 4
Name Meaning: God is gracious, gift of God
Patron Saint of: Priests, confessors.

St. Joseph

aint Joseph was by birth of the royal
family of David, but was living in humble
obscurity as a carpenter when God raised
him to the highest sanctity, and chose him to be the
spouse of His Virgin Mother, and foster-father and
guardian to Jesus.

Joseph, says Holy Scripture, was a just man; he
was innocent and pure, and became the husband of
Mary, he was gentle and tender, as one worthy to be
named the father of Jesus. When he learned that Mary
carried within her womb the Lord of heaven, he feared

to take her as his wife, but an angel told him not to fear, and all doubts vanished.

When Herod sought the life of the divine Infant, an angel told Joseph in a dream to flee with the Child and His Mother into Egypt. Joseph at once arose and obeyed. Being directed by God in another vision he returned to the land of Herod Antipas, in Galilee, to his former home in Nazareth. When Jesus was a little older Joseph and Mary found him in the temple after being missing for three days. When Mary asked him why He had done this to them Jesus replied, "Did you not know that I must be about my Fathers business"? Even though he stayed in the temple unknown to His parents, in the end He was still obedient to them.

There is no further mention of St. Joseph in scripture after this and he is presumed to have died before the marriage of Cana and the beginning of Jesus' ministry. We can imagine the happiness of Jesus and Mary attending to his death praying by him and comforting him in his last moments.

Feast Day: March 19
Name Meaning: He Shall Add
Patron Saint of: Families, Carpenters, Married Couples, Laborers, House Seekers, The Universal Church, A Happy Death.

St. Juan Diego

Cuauhtlatzin (translated eagle that speaks) was born July 12, 1474 in Cuautitlan of the Texcoco Kingdom. In 1524 Franciscan missionaries came to Mexico and Cuauhtlatzin and his wife requested to be baptized, receiving on that day their Christian names, Juan Diego and Maria Lucia. Five years later, Maria Lucia died and Juan Diego was left with his elderly uncle, Juan Bernardino in Tulpetlac.

Every Saturday and Sunday Juan Diego walked nine miles for religious instruction and Mass.

On Saturday, December 9, 1531, as he walked he heard singing on the top of Tepeyac Hill.

As he climbed to see who was singing, he received his first vision of the Blessed Virgin Mary.

She asked Juan Diego to deliver a message to the Bishop that a church should be built on the place she was standing. Juan Diego delivered this message but the Bishop could not believe that Mary would appear to this simple peasant and send him with this message. On the fourth apparition, Mary sent proof to the Bishop that she truly wanted a church built on the spot she had shown to Juan Diego. As he knelt before the Bishop and opened his tilma, flowers that were rare for that part of the country fell to the ground and the image of Our Lady appeared on the rough surface of the cloth. The Bishop and those who had doubted Juan Diego fell to their knees. The church was built and Juan Diego received permission from the Bishop to live as a hermit in a small hut on Tepeyac Hill.

He cared for the church and for the first pilgrims who came to pray to Our Lady of Guadalupe and to see her image on the tilma. He died May 30, 1548.

Juan Diego was canonized July 31, 2002 by Pope John Paul II.

Feast Day: December 9.

St. Jude the Apostle

Saint Jude was one of the original apostles and is also known as Thaddeus. He is the author of the canonical epistle and describes himself as Jude, the servant of Jesus Christ and brother of James the Less. The term could also mean "brethren of the Lord" describing their closeness with Jesus.

The epistle he authored is directed to the Churches of the East, particularly to the Jewish Converts.

Tradition asserts that Jude the Apostle preached in Mesopotamia, Syria, Samaria and Persia. According to

Eusebius, he returned to Jerusalem in the year 62AD and assisted in the election of James as bishop of Jerusalem. He then left to spread the Word of Christ to Persia and suffered martyrdom in Armenia which was part of the Persian empire.

In time St. Jude came to be regarded as the special patron of "hopeless cases", possibly because it was felt that devotion to him had been neglected for some time, most likely because of his name being the same as the traitor Judas. A little office of St. Jude appeared and in abbreviated form, the main prayer reads: "Most Holy apostle, most faithful friend and servant of Jesus Christ, Jude Thaddeus, who... is invoked as the special advocate of those who are in trouble and almost without hope... pray for me that by your merits, I may receive consolation in my tribulations and difficulties... and finally, with you and all the elect, I may love and bless God eternally. Amen.

Feast Day: October 28
Name Meaning: Gentleness of character
Patron Saint of: Desperate situations, forgotten causes, hospital workers, hospitals, impossible causes.

Kateri Tekakwitha

Kateri Tekakwitha was born near the town of Auriesville, NY in 1656. She was the daughter of a Mohawk warrior and a Catholic Algonquin woman. When she was four, her mom, dad and brother died when smallpox swept through their village. Tekakwitha was left partially blind and her face scarred. She was adopted by her two aunts and her uncle and moved to a new settlement called Caughnawaga.

Tekakwitha worked in the fields with her aunts and gathered roots in the forests for medicines and dye.

She collected firewood and helped with the everyday chores around the house. When Tekakwitha was eighteen, a Jesuit Missionary came to the village and she was allowed religious instruction. At the age of twenty, she was baptized and given the name Kateri, but her faith was not accepted by her family. She was refused food and threatened and chastised until she finally fled to a Catholic mission in Canada.

At St. Francis Xavier she dedicated her life to prayer and penance and caring for the sick and aged.

She made crosses out of sticks and placed them throughout the woods to remind herself to take time for prayer. She had great devotion to the Blessed Sacrament. She received her First Communion on Christmas day, 1677. People in the village loved listening to her stories about Jesus and felt close to God when they spent time with her. She took a vow of chastity in 1679 and hoped to start a convent for Native American sisters but her poor health prevented her from fulfilling that dream. She died in 1680 at the age of 24. It was told that moments after her death, the scars on her face miraculously disappeared.

She was beatified by Pope John Paul II in 1980.

Feast Day: July 14
Patron Saint of: Ecology, environment, loss of parents, people in exile.

St. Lawrence Martyr

Saint Lawrence who was born in Spain in the third century became one of the seven deacons of Rome and eventually archdeacon to Pope St. Sixtus II. He was the distributor of alms, and "keeper of the treasures of the church" in a time when Christianity was outlawed.

After Pope St. Sixtus II was condemned to death, he predicted that St. Lawrence would be martyred three days after him. The pope and the other six deacons were beheaded, leaving Lawrence as the ranking Church official in Rome.

In preparation, of his death St. Lawrence sold many of the Church's possessions and donated the money to the poor. When the prefect of Rome heard of this, he demanded from Lawrence all the treasures of the Church. St. Lawrence presented to the prefect all the blind, crippled, poor and orphans and said, "Here are the true treasures of the Church; they convert our alms into imperishable treasure for us. Furious, the prefect sentenced, St. Lawrence to be tied to a red hot griddle and burned to death. St. Lawrence not only bore the agony, but in the middle of his torment instructed the executioner to turn him over, as he was broiled enough on the one side.

It is said that when the remains of St. Stephen the Protomartyr were moved to the tomb of St. Lawrence, St. Lawrence's lifeless body moved aside and extended a hand of welcome to the body of St. Stephen.

Feast Day: August 10
Name Meaning: The laurel crowned one
Patron Saint of: Cooks, school children, seminarians, deacons, armourers, archivists,cutlers, comics, students, vintners, poor people.

St. Louis de Montfort

ouis Marie Grignion was born in 1673 at Montfort, France. At the age of twelve, he went to study at the Jesuit college at Rennes, where he made frequent visits before the Blessed Sacrament. He listened to stories from the local priest of his life as a missionary, which encouraged Louis to pursue his vocation. At age nineteen, he walked to Paris to study theology and along the way gave away all he owned to the poor.

He was ordained in 1700 and was assigned as chaplain to the hospital in Poitiers.

There he met Blessed Marie Louise Trichet who would later help him to organize the Daughters of Divine Wisdom known for the teaching of children and the care of the poor.

Louis Marie traveled to Rome where Pope Clement XI appointed him Apostolic Missionary, sending him back to France. He preached in the missions from Brittany to Nantes. His success caused great controversy and attempts were made to kill him.

He worked hard to further devotion to the Blessed Mother through the rosary. He wrote the books True Devotion to the Blessed Mother, the Secret of the Rosary and the Secret of Mary. In 1715, he organized the Company of Mary (the Montfort Fathers), a missionary group of priests, and along with Blessed Marie Louise Trichet opened a school in La Rochelle. The following year he died at Saint-Laurent-sur-Sevre. He was canonized in 1947.

Feast Day: April 28
Name Meaning: Famous Warrior
Patron Saint of: Preachers.

St. Lucy

The mother of St. Lucy suffered four years from a blood disease, and the help of doctors failed. St. Lucy reminded her mother that a woman in the Gospel had been healed of the same disorder.

"St. Agatha," she said "stands ever in the sight of Christ for whom she died. "Only touch her sepulchre with faith, and you will be healed."

They spent the night praying by her tomb, until overcome by weariness, both fell asleep. St. Agatha appeared in a vision to St. Lucy, and calling her sister, foretold of her mother's recovery and her own martyrdom. That instant the cure went into effect and in her gratitude St. Lucy's mother allowed her daughter to distribute her wealth among the poor, and consecrate her life to Christ.

A young man to whom she had been promised in marriage accused her of being a Christian to the pagans; but Our Lord, by a special miracle, saved this virgin, whom He had chosen for His own.

The authorities ordered that she be burned to death but the fire burning around her did not harm her. Then a sword was plunged into her heart, and the promise made at the tomb of St. Agatha was fulfilled.

Feast Day: December 13
Name Meaning: The Bringer of Light
Patron Saint of: Eye Problems, Blindness, Hemorrhage, Lamplighters.

postle, Martyr, Patron of Physicians and Painters although not an apostle in the strict sense (he was not one of the original 12 mentioned in Matthew 10:2-4), St. Luke is commonly considered an apostle nonetheless, and is the only Gentile to have his writings accepted as part of the New Testament. He worked as a medical doctor, in Antioch before being converted by St. Paul. St. Luke became his disciple and companion during many of St. Paul's missions. Everything we know about the Incarnation, birth and childhood of Our Lord comes to us from St. Luke. During the time that St. Paul was imprisoned in Rome, St. Luke wrote the Acts of the Apostles, in order to leave an accurate account of their activities up until that time.

As the ox or calf were used in Jewish sacrifices, these became the symbols of St. Luke, because his writing dwelt particularly on the sacrificial aspect of our Lord's atonement, and on His Divine Priesthood. He remained with St. Paul until his martyrdom and then went to preach in Italy, France and Macedonia.

Whether he died the death of a martyr is not clear among ancient church writers but his remains are kept in the church of the Holy Apostles in Constantinople.

St. Luke is also credited as having painted the first likenesses of the Blessed Virgin Mary and of Christ.

Feast Day: October 18
Name Meaning: The Bringer of Light
Patron Saint of: Doctors, Physicians, Glass Makers, Butchers, Sculptors.

St. Margaret Mary

Saint Margaret Mary was born in 1647 at Janots, a small town of the Burgundy area in France. She was the fifth of seven children. Her Father was a well to do notary and the family owned a country house with farmland and they also had some connections to the aristocracy. Her father died of pneumonia when Margaret was eight years old, putting the family in a tough situation because he had spent most of the families' money. Margaret was then sent away to a convent school where she loved the way of life which the Urbanist Sisters lived and taught. The nuns were so impressed with her devotion to Christ that they allowed her to make her first communion years earlier than was the norm. She then came down with a sickness that kept her bedridden for four years at home. During this time she and her Mother went through a tough time with her father's relatives who were trying to take over his estate. They treated them like servants, but thankfully her older brother then came of age and regained control of the properties. At twenty Margaret was inspired by a vision and entered a convent and at twenty-two made her profession with the nuns of the Order of the Visitation founded by St. Francis De Sales. As the years passed in the convent Margaret Mary began experiencing supernatural events beginning with hearing the Lord inviting her to take the place which St. John had occupied at the Last Supper. He told her that the love of his heart must spread and manifest itself to man and he would reveal its graces through her. Jesus would reveal things to her over the next eighteen months. She was at first not believed and was called delusional by her superiors. However one Jesuit, Father Claude de la Colombiere believed her. He died at the convent a few years later, but his writings of her convinced many, and so she and her visions were finally accepted. When she was 43 she fell ill and received the last Sacraments before she passed. She made the devotion to the Sacred Heart of Jesus spread around the world and her "Twelve Promises of Jesus" and other revelations are cornerstones of devotion to Jesus and His Sacred Heart.

Feast Day: October 16

Name Meaning: The pearl

Patron Saint of: Against polio, polio parents, devotees to the Sacred Heart, loss of parents.

St. Maria Goretti

Saint Maria Goretti was born in Corinaldo, Italy in 1890. Her parents, Luigi and Assunta, had seven children, the oldest dying when he was only a few months old.

When the small farm they lived on could no longer support their family, they moved to the small town of Nettuno and joined with Giovanni Serenelli and his son, Alessandro as sharecroppers on a farm owned by Count Mazzoleni.

Times were extremely difficult, sharing an old cheese dairy with Assunta having to do the cleaning, cooking and mending for her own family as well as the Serenellis.

When Luigi died in 1901 of malaria complicated by pneumonia, Assunta had to take over his job in the fields and Maria had to do all of the work at home.

Although she was only eleven, Maria filled her day with work and prayer. She prayed the rosary daily with the other children just as her father had done before he died. She made her First Communion a year early, dedicating herself to learning the catechism.

Alessandro began making advances at Maria and threatening her if she told anyone. On July 5, 1902, Maria was attacked by Allessandro. When she refused him and insisted that God wouldn't want this and he would go to hell, he stabbed her repeatedly.

She was taken to the hospital and before dying the following day, she met with the parish priest of Nettuno and forgave Alessandro completely.

The superior of the hospital made her a Child of Mary and she died wearing a medal of Our Lady and holding a crucifix. While in prison, Alessandro had a vision of Maria which changed his entire life.

He and Maria's mother, Assunta, were present at her canonization by Pope Pius XII in 1950.

Feast Day: July 6
Name Meaning: beloved; love
Patron Saint of: Youth, children of Mary, teenage girls, rape victims.

St. Mark the Evangelist

Saint Mark, one of the four evangelists, was converted to the faith by St. Peter. According to Saint Bede, he was of the race of Aaron, converted by the apostles after Christ's resurrection. He was the disciple and interpreter of St. Peter and St. Jerome states that he is the same Mark whom St. Peter, in his first Epistle, calls his son.

It is said that he wrote his Gospel in Italy at the request of the Romans, probably before the year 49 of the Christian era. At that time, Alexandria in Egypt was ranked the second city of the world.

St. Peter sent his disciple there and appointed him bishop of that city, so he could evangelize the citizens there. According to his Acts, which appear to have been written in Egypt, in the fourth and fifth centuries, he landed at Cyrene, in a part of Libya. By numerous miracles he converted many pagans, and demolished several temples of idols. He also carried the Gospel into Thebais and other parts of Egypt. Twelve years were spent by St. Mark preaching in various parts of the country before he entered Alexandria, where he converted many to Christianity. Mark had to flee the persecutions that started against him but he first ordained St. Anianus bishop before leaving. After two years he again visited his Church of Alexandria, but soon thereafter departed for Rome.

He then returned to Alexandria and, after some time, was apprehended on the feast of the god Serapis, dragged over the ground the whole day and at night thrown into prison. The next day he was again dragged as before, until he died on April 25th, in the year 68.

The body of the Saint is preserved in Venice, where a great basilica is dedicated to his honor.

Feast Day: April 25
Name Meaning: The little hammer
Patron Saint of: Attorneys, barristers, captives, against impenitence, notaries, stained glass workers.

aint John tells us that "Jesus loved Martha and Mary and Lazarus." In his gospel, John tells us of the special relationship Jesus had with Martha, her sister, and her brother.

Evidently, Jesus was a regular guest at Martha's home in Bethany, a small town just outside Jerusalem. There are references of three visits in scripture: Luke 10:38-42, John 11:1-53, and John 12:1-9.

It is easy to identify with Martha, as Luke portrays her in his Gospel. Martha welcomes Jesus and his apostles into her home and does whatever she can to serve them. Martha shows her frustration with her sister Mary who does not help, but instead sits down to listen to Jesus. Martha asks Jesus to intervene but Jesus reminds her that only one thing is truly important, and that is listening to him.

The next time Martha sees Jesus she is grieving the death of her brother Lazarus, with a house full of mourners, when she hears that Jesus is in the area.

She immediately leaves her guests and goes to find him. Her conversation with Jesus shows her faith.

She clearly states without doubt that she believes in Jesus' power, in the resurrection, and also that Jesus is the Son of God. He tells her that He is the Resurrection and the Life and He then goes on to raise Lazarus from the dead. The last image of Martha in the Bible is when Jesus returns to Bethany to share a meal with His friends. We hear the controversy that the raising of Lazarus has caused.

We also read of how Mary caused a commotion over her using an expensive perfume to anoint Jesus.

What we read about Martha is that she spent much of her time in service to Christ. After the Pentecost it is said that Martha accompanied Mary on a boat with no sails or oars and the boat was taken to France where they spent the rest of their lives evangelizing.

Feast Day: July 29
Name Meaning: The lady
Patron Saint of: Housewives, cooks, restaurants, hosts.

St. Martin de Porres

Saint Martin de Porres was born in Lima, Peru in 1579. He was the illegitimate son of a Spanish knight and a freed Panama slave. His mother apprenticed him to a surgeon/barber where he learned to care for the sick.

When he was fifteen, Martin became a lay helper at the Dominican Friary of Lima. After nine years of service, his continuous prayer, penance and charity led the community to request that he join their order. Martin continued to care for the sick and for slaves brought over from Africa. He helped to open an orphanage and a hospital. He became known as a skilled surgeon and healer, saving the life of a priest with a badly infected leg and healing the fingers of a student working to become a priest. His cures came as much from his prayers as they did from his medical knowledge. He was known to heal the sick outside the friary with as little as a glass of water.

He ran an animal hospital at his sister's house.

Stories are told of him having a cat, a dog, and a mouse eating together from the same bowl of food.

He had a reputation for spiritual wisdom which caused people to come to him to solve marriage problems and resolve theological conflicts.

Martin was known to have the gift of bi-location and levitation during prayer. He was said to have been seen in Mexico, Central America, and Japan by people who knew him well, even though he had not left Lima since joining the order. He appeared at the bedside of those suffering without being asked.

His fellow Dominicans referred to him as the father of charity. He died November 3, 1639 and was canonized by Pope John XXIII in 1962.

Feast Day: November 3
Name Meaning: of Mars, Warlike
Patron Saint of: Barbers, hairdressers, social justice.

St. Martin of Tours

Saint Martin of Tours, Bishop, Patron of France, was the son of a pagan Roman officer in what is now Hungary. In Amiens, one cold night, he gave his cloak to a freezing beggar, and later saw in a vision that it was really Jesus. St. Martin was the uncle of St. Patrick of Ireland.

He became a disciple of St. Hilary of Poitiers and converted his mother, but his father remained a pagan. St. Martin was active in fighting against Arianism and was publicly scourged and banished for his efforts. He lived as a hermit for ten years, and attracted followers that he organized into the first monastery in France. In 372 he was made Bishop of Tours. He destroyed pagan temples, often miraculously and was often saved from harm by miraculous means. He raised 3 persons from the dead and cured two lepers, one so far gone with the disease that the miracle converted many of the witnesses. Two thousand monks and nuns came to his funeral. There are 500 villages in France named after him.

Feast Day: November 11
Name Meaning: The warlike one
Patron Saint of: Against poverty, alcoholism, soldiers, tailors, cavalry, innkeepers, hotel keepers.

St. Mary Magdalene

Of the earlier life of Mary Magdalene we know only that she was "a woman who was a sinner." From the depth of her degradation she raised her eyes to Jesus with sorrow, hope, and love.

She said not a word, but bathed His feet with her tears, wiped them with the hair of her head, kissed them in humility, and at their touch her sins and her stain were gone and his own divine lips gave her absolution, and bade her go in peace. She stood with Our Lady and St. John at the foot of the cross, the representative of the many who have had much forgiven. To her first, after His blessed Mother, and through her to His apostles, Our Lord gave the certainty of His resurrection; and to her first He made Himself known, calling her by her name, because she was His friend. The cave in which St. Mary lived for thirty years is still seen, and the chapel on the mountain-top, in which she was caught up daily, like St. Paul, to "visions and revelations of the Lord".

When her end drew near she was drawn to a spot still marked by a "sacred pillar," where the holy Bishop Maximin awaited her, and when she had received her Lord, she peacefully fell asleep in death.

Feast Day: July 22
Name Meaning: The Penitent
Patron Saint of: Pharmacists, Perfumers, Converts, Hairdressers, Penitent Men.

St. Matthew the Apostle

One day, as Our Lord was walking by the Sea of Galilee, He saw Matthew the publican, whose business it was to collect the taxes from the people for their Roman masters.

Jesus said to him, "Follow Me;" and leaving all, Matthew arose and followed Him.

Since the publicans were disliked by the Jews as enemies of their country, no Pharisee would sit with one at a table. Our Savior alone had compassion for them. So St. Matthew made a great feast, to which he invited Jesus and His disciples, with a number of these publicans, who then eagerly listened to Him.

It was then, in answer to the murmurs of the Pharisees, that He said, "They that are healthy do not need a physician. I have not come to call the just, but the sinners to penance."

After the Ascension, St. Matthew remained some years in Judaea, and there wrote his gospel, to teach his countrymen that Jesus was their true Lord and King, foretold by the prophets. St. Matthew afterward preached the Faith far and wide, and is said to have finished his life's work in Parthia.

Feast Day: September 21
Name Meaning: The Gift of the Lord
Patron Saint of: Accountants, Bookkeepers, Bankers, Tax Collectors, Security Guards, Stock Brokers.

St. Maximilian Kolbe

Saint Maximilian was born in 1894 in Russian occupied Poland. He entered the Franciscan junior seminary in 1907 and became a novice in the Conventual Franciscan Order at 16, making temporary vows in 1911.

While studying philosophy and theology in Rome, he and six friends founded the Immaculata Movement to spread devotion to Our Lady.

Returning to Poland after his ordination in 1918, he began the publication of the magazine "The Knight of the Immaculata".

His work soon outgrew the friaries and he founded the new monastery of Niepokalanow, the "Cities of the Immaculate". Here he published more magazines and papers and started a radio program.

Maximilian opened similar monasteries in Japan and India before returning home in 1936 due to poor health. By 1939, his monastery housed almost 800 men and was totally self-sufficient. He and several brothers were arrested during a Nazi invasion but were released and returned to their work.

However, in 1941, Maximilian was arrested again and sent to the concentration camp at Auschwitz.

He was assigned to a work group with other priests and his dedication to the faith and calm demeanor caused him the worst jobs and the most beatings.

Near the end of July, a group of ten men were chosen to be executed in exchange for one prisoner who had escaped.

When Francis Gajowniczek, a young husband and father was chosen, he cried out in despair.

Maximilian volunteered to take his place and after weeks of starvation, dehydration, and neglect, he was given an injection of carbonic acid. He died August 14, 1941 and was canonized by Pope John Paul II in 1982.

Feast Day: August 14
Name Meaning: Greatest
Patron Saint of: Drug addiction, families, journalists, prisoners, pro-life movement.

St. Michael the Archangel

Saint Michael is one of the seven archangels. His stories are made known to us through Scripture. In the Old Testament book of Daniel, Michael is referred to as one of the chief princes. Michael comes to aid and to comfort Daniel and is represented as the protector of the people of Israel during the Babylonian Exile.

The New Testament Epistle of St. Jude reveals the dispute between Michael and the devil over Moses' body. While warning against false teachers in our communities, St. Jude notes that even Michael leaves the judgment of the devil to the Lord. Finally, in Revelation, we are told of a great battle in Heaven between Michael with his angels and the dragon.

Michael is seen as overpowering the dragon, which loses its' place in Heaven. Because of this victory over evil, St. Michael is believed to be the protector of all Christians against the devil, especially at the hour of our death. He can protect us in any of our daily battles. In art, St. Michael the archangel is typically shown standing over the dragon or some image of the devil, in full armor with sword and shield. He holds perfectly balanced scales symbolizing his role, during judgment, of weighing the souls of the departed.

Feast Day: September 29
Name Meaning: He Who is Like God
Patron Saint of: Policemen, Knights, Paratroopers, Grocers, Those in Battle, Radiologists.

St. Monica

Saint Monica, the mother of St. Augustine was born in Northern Africa in the year 333 AD. She was married early in life to a pagan official. His mother lived with them and that was hard on Monica because they both had bad tempers. They had three children together of which Augustine was the eldest, Navigius was another son and Perpetua was the daughter. At first her husband did not consent to have their children baptized.

Through her patience and prayers her husband and his mother finally converted to the Catholic faith in the year 370. He died shortly after his conversion and Monica refused to marry again. Her two younger children then were free to enter the religious life and did so. However, her son Augustine was much more difficult. He had become a heretic. She was very distraught and continued to pray and weep for him for 17 years. She constantly asked clergy to pray for him with her, to a point that they would try to avoid her because of her persistence at this seemingly hopeless endeavor. A certain Holy Bishop consoled her by telling her "It is not possible that the son of so many tears shall perish." Monica even pursued Augustine to Rome, but when she arrived he had left to Milan.

She kept following, and at Milan found St. Ambrose and through him she was able to finally see Augustine convert and be baptized by St. Ambrose in the year 387. St Monica died later that same year on her way back to Africa from Rome in the Italian town of Ostia. She was buried there for centuries until her relics were brought to Rome where many miracles occurred along the way.

Feast Day: August 27
Name Meaning: The wise counselor
Patron Saint of: Abuse victims, alcoholics, homemakers, married women, mothers, victims of adultery, widows, disappointing children.

Mother Teresa

other Teresa was born Agnes Gonxha Bojaxhiy on August 26, 1910 in Macedonia. At age 18, she became a postulant with the Loretto sisters in Ireland. She was sent to India in 1929 and made her final profession in 1937.

She taught at St. Mary's School in Calcutta for several years before she received what she called "a call within a call".

"I was to leave the convent and help the poor while living among them. It was an order. To fail would have been to break the faith.

"Asking permission to care for the poor in the city, Mother Teresa changed to a sari as a dress and, barefooted, began teaching the children in the slums and caring for the dying. As young women began to join her in ministry, a new congregation emerged.

In 1950, Pope Pius XII formally approved the Order of the Missionaries of Charity. Mother Teresa expanded the missions throughout India, Europe, Africa, Australia, the Middle East, London, and North America.

In 1971, she was awarded the Pope John XXIII Peace Prize and in 1979, the Nobel Peace prize.

By the 1980's and 1990's, Mother Teresa had opened houses in almost all Communist nations. Despite her failing health, she continued to travel and speak on the rights of the poor. The sisters of her congregation numbered nearly 4,000 and she had 610 foundations in 123 countries. She returned home in July 1997 and died at her Motherhouse in September.

Pope John Paul II beatified Mother Teresa on October 19, 2003. In his homily, he referred to her as a "diminutive woman in love with God, a humble Gospel messenger and a tireless benefactor of humanity."

He said, "Thus was Mother Teresa 'bringing souls to God and God to souls' and satisfying Christ's thirst, especially for those most in need, those whose vision of God had been dimmed by suffering and pain."

Feast Day: September 15
Name Meaning: To harvest.

St. Nicholas

Saint Nicholas, was born toward the end of the third century. His uncle, the Archbishop of Myra in Lycia, ordained him a priest, and appointed him abbot of a monastery; and on the death of the Archbishop he was elected Bishop of the vacant See. Throughout his life he retained the bright manners of his early years, and showed himself the special protector of the innocent and the wronged.

Nicholas once heard that a person who had fallen into poverty intended to abandon his three daughters to a life of sin.

Determined, if possible, to save their innocence, the Saint went out by night, and, taking with him a bag of gold, flung it into the window of the sleeping father and hurried off.

He, on awaking, deemed the gift a godsend, and with it dowered his eldest child. The Saint, overjoyed at his success, did the same for the second daughter; but the third time, as he stole away, the father, who was watching, overtook him and kissed his feet, saying: "Nicholas, why do you conceal yourself from me? You are my helper, and the one who has delivered my soul and my daughters' from hell."

St. Nicholas is usually represented by the side of a barrel, where a certain man had concealed the bodies of his three children whom he had killed, but who were restored to life by the Saint. He died A.D. 342.

His relics were transferred in 1807, to Bari, Italy, and there, after fifteen centuries, "the manna of St. Nicholas" still flows from his bones and heals all kinds of sicknesses.

Feast Day: December 6
Name Meaning: The Victorious People
Patron Saint of: Children, Fishermen, Merchants, Sailors, Bakers, Dock Workers.

St. Padre Pio

adre Pio was born Francesco Forgione in Pietrelcina Italy in the year 1887. His family lived on a farm and were shepherds. At the age of 16 he entered the novitiate of the Capuchin Franciscan Friars and was ordained when he was 20.

After going home for a while because of health problems he was sent to the friary of San Giovanni Rotondo where he remained for the rest of his life. While praying before a crucifix on September 20, 1918 he received the stigmata wounds of Christ and was the first priest ever to be so blessed.

168

As word spread of this holy priest, especially by American soldiers coming home from WWII with stories about Padre Pio, he himself became the center of pilgrimage for both the powerful and the curious.

He heard confessions for hours and is said to have been able to read the consciences of those who held back from telling him some sins. He was also said to be blessed with the ability to bilocate, levitate and heal the sick with his touch and prayer.

It is said that he foretold of John Paul II's papacy when the future pope was a young priest visiting Padre Pio. He founded a hospital that cares for over 60,000 people a year and founded prayer groups that continue today. He died in 1968 and was canonized in 2002 by Pope John Paul II. Many miracles and cures have been found to be attributed to the intercession of Padre Pio.

Feast Day: September 23
Name Meaning: The pious one.

St. Pancracio

ancracio (Pancras) was born in Phrygia around 289 to parents of Roman origin. His mother died during childbirth and his father died when Pancracio was eight, leaving him in the care of his uncle Dionysius. They moved to Rome where Pancracio was converted to Christianity.

The legend is told that Pancracio gave all his possessions to the poor which drew notice to his Christianity during the persecution of Christians by Diocletian. He was placed before authorities and asked to perform sacrifices to the Roman gods to which he refused. He was promised power and wealth if he would deny his Christianity but again he refused. Thus, the Emperor had him beheaded on the Via Aurelia at the age of fourteen.

Pope Symmachus had a Basilica, the Basilica of San Pancrazio, built over the place where he was buried. Some of his relics were sent to England as a part of an effort toward evangelization and St. Augustine of Canterbury dedicated his first church to this martyr.

It is said that one of the oldest Christian sites of worship in England is St. Pancras Old Church.

Pancracio is often shown with a sword in his images because of his association with two soldiers, Sts. Nereus and Achilleus, who died in the same persecution. He is invoked against cramps, false witness, perjury and headaches.

Feast Day: May 12
Patron Saint of: Children, teens.

St. Patrick

Saint Patrick was born towards the close of the fourth century, in a village called Bonaven Taberniae, which seems to be the town of Kilpatrick, on the mouth of the river Clyde, in Scotland. In his sixteenth year he was carried into captivity by barbarians, who took him into Ireland, where he was forced to shepherd cattle in the mountains.

After six months spent in slavery under the same master, St. Patrick was advised by God in a dream to return to his own country. Some years afterwards he was again made captive, but regained his freedom after two months. When he was at home with his parents, God revealed to him, many visions, that He destined him to the great work of the conversion of Ireland. He left his family and consecrated his soul to God, to carry His name to the ends of the earth.

He went to Ireland, to preach the gospel, where the worship of idols still generally was practiced.

He devoted himself entirely to the salvation of these pagans. He traveled over the whole island, where he baptized an infinite number of people and instituted monastic life. St. Patrick used the shamrock to preach the meaning of the Trinity and its three persons in one doctrine. Legend also tells us that St. Patrick drove all the snakes off Ireland. He took nothing from the many thousands whom he baptized. He died and was buried at Down in Ulster. His body was found there in a church of his name in 1185.

Feast Day: March 17
Name Meaning: The Noble One
Patron Saint of: Ireland, Snakebites.

St. Paul the Apostle

Saint Paul was born at Tarsus, of Jewish parents, and studied at Jerusalem. While still a young man, he trained in the schools of the Pharisees and saw Christians as enemies.

He had letters from the high-priest of Jerusalem, authorizing him to search for Christians and bring them before Jewish courts. He stood by and watched those who stoned the martyr Stephen, and in his angry state he pressed on to Damascus, "persecuting the disciples of Christ." But near Damascus a light from heaven struck him to the earth.

He heard a voice which said, "Why are you persecuting me? He saw the form of Christ, and then for three days he saw nothing more. He awoke from his trance a new man, a new person in Jesus Christ.

He left Damascus for a long retreat in Arabia, and then, at the call of God, he carried the Gospel to the uttermost limits of the world, and for years he lived and labored with no thought but of the thought of Christ crucified, no desire but to spend and be spent for Him.

He became the apostle of the Gentiles. With St. Peter he consecrated Rome, our holy city, by his martyrdom, and poured into its Church all his doctrine with all his blood. He left fourteen Epistles, which have been a fountain-head of the Church's doctrine.

Feast Day: June 29
Name Meaning: The Small One
Patron Saint of: Authors, Lay People, Evangelists, Reporters, Publishers.

St. Peregrine

aint Peregrine was born in Forli, Italy around 1265, at that time, Forli was governed by the Pope as part of the Papal States. Peregrine grew up in a family which was actively involved in the opposition or anti-papal party. Because of anti-papal political activity, the city was under the church penalty of interdict which meant that Mass and the Sacraments could not be celebrated in the city. St. Philip Benizi was sent to Forli to preach the reconciliation of the city and the removal of the penalty. Young Peregrine was so intense in his political fervor that he heckled Philip during the preaching and at one point Peregrine struck St. Philip. The moment of striking St. Philip seemed to drastically change Peregrine. He began to channel his energies into good works and eventually he joined the Servants of Mary and pronounced his vows in the Servite Priory in Siena, Italy. Peregrine then returned to Forli, where he spent the rest of his life. He especially dedicated himself to the sick, the poor and the fringe people of society. He also imposed a special penance on himself to stand whenever it was not necessary to sit. This led to varicose veins. The varicose veins deteriorated into an open, running sore on his leg. The open, running sore was diagnosed as cancer. The wound became so obvious, odorous and painful that the local surgeon scheduled surgery to amputate the leg. Suddenly Peregrine had given himself to people in similar situations and then found he must lean on his own faith in the goodness of God. The night before the operation he prayed before the image of the crucified Christ in the priory chapter room. At the age of 60 he was challenged to carry a new and more difficult cross. His prayer led him into deep trance-like sleep during which he envisioned the crucified Christ leaving the cross and touching his cancerous leg. When Peregrine awakened from the trance of prayer, he discovered the wound healed and the leg saved. St. Peregrine lived 20 more years. He died on May 1, 1345 at the age of 80. He was canonized on December 27, 1726.

Feast Day: May 2

Name Meaning: The pilgrim

Patron Saint of: Cancer, cancer patients, breast cancer, sick people, AIDS sufferers, skin diseases.

St. Peter the Apostle

eter was of Bethsaida in Galilee, and as he was fishing one day, he was called by Our Lord to be one of His apostles. He was poor and uneducated, but candid, eager, and loving.

In his heart, first of all, grew conviction, and from his lips came confession. "You are the Christ, the Son of the living God;" and so Our Lord chose him, and chose him to be the Rock of His Church, His Vicar on earth, the head and prince of His apostles, the center and very principle of the Church's oneness, the source of all spiritual powers, and the unerring teacher of

His truth. All Scripture is alive with him; but after Pentecost he stands out in the full grandeur of his office. He fills the vacant apostolic throne, admits the Jews by thousands into the fold, opens it to the Gentiles in the person of Cornelius; founds, and for a time rules, the Church at Antioch, and sends Mark to found the Church of Alexandria.

Ten years after the Ascension he went to Rome, the center of the majestic Roman Empire, where were gathered all the glories and the wealth of the earth and all the powers of evil.

There he established his Chair, and for twenty-five years labored with St. Paul in building up the great Roman Church. He was crucified by order of Nero, and buried on the Vatican Hill. He wrote two epistles, and suggested and approved the Gospel of St. Mark.

Feast Day: June 29
Name Meaning: The Rock
Patron Saint of: Fisherman, Masons, Bridge Builders, Ship Builders, Clockmakers.

St. Peter Julian Eymard

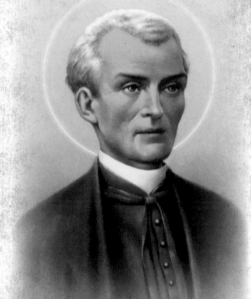

Peter Julian was born in 1811 in LaMure, France. His family was poor and did not want him to pursue a religious vocation.

At eighteen, despite opposition and ill health, Peter Julian went to seminary and was ordained in 1834.

He had a great devotion to Mary and loved to visit the Marian Shrines. After five years as a parish priest, he joined the Marist Fathers.

He served as Provincial at Lyon and worked tirelessly to promote Forty Hour devotion to the Blessed Sacrament in parishes.

While carrying the Blessed Sacrament on the feast of Corpus Christi, Peter Julian experienced an overwhelming love of Christ in the Eucharist.

He asked for permission to leave the Marist Order and he prepared to establish the Blessed Sacrament Fathers, dedicated to Perpetual Adoration.

He worked to prepare others to receive First Communion, especially adults coming back to the Catholic Church. The archbishop of Paris was interested in the group because of the active work they were doing with those who had been away from the Church as well as their evangelization to new Catholics. Due to extreme poverty, few were interested in joining the congregation. But once he gained the attention of Pope Pius IX, his order grew. In 1858, he founded a community of sisters known as the Servants of the Blessed Sacrament and later formed associations of priests and laypeople committed to pray an hour a day in the presence of Christ in the Tabernacle.

Peter Julian died in 1868. He was canonized in 1962, the day after the end of the first session of Vatican II by Pope John XXIII.

Feast Day: August 2
Name Meaning: Rock
Patron Saint of: Christian Schools.

St. Philip

Philip was born in Bethsaida in Galilee. After Jesus called Peter and Andrew to be His Apostles, He found Philip and said, "Follow me."

Philip left all he had and all he was doing and did as Jesus said. In the Gospel of John, Philip then finds Nathanael and tells him, "We have found the one about whom Moses wrote in the law, and also the prophets, Jesus, son of Joseph from Nazareth."

He persuades Nathanael to "Come and see".

Jesus turned to Philip during the miracle of the

loaves and fishes and asked him where to buy bread to feed the multitude.

Philip tells him that they do not have money to buy enough bread to feed the entire crowd.

But again, we see that Jesus knows Philip will follow his instructions. Later, Philip is approached by some Greeks who want him to take them to see Jesus but he goes and gets Andrew and together they find Jesus and tell him. Philip remains trustworthy and dedicated to Jesus. Finally, during the Last Supper we hear him say to Jesus, "Master, show us the Father and that will be enough for us," giving Jesus the opportunity to teach us of the unity between He and His Father. Tradition teaches that after the Ascension, Philip preached in Phrygia. He went on to spread the Gospel in Hierapolis with his sister Mariamme and Bartholomew. Because of the conversion of the proconsul of the city, the three were tortured.

Philip and Bartholomew were hung upside down to be crucified but because Philip continued to teach the people from the cross, they released Bartholomew but Philip asked to remain. He died in c.80.

Feast Day: May 3
Name Meaning: Lover of Horses
Patron Saint of: Uruguay, hatters, pastry chefs.

St. Philomena

Very little is known about the life of Saint Philomena, except through private revelations which mystics have had from this saint. What we know for sure is that she lived in the early days of the church and was martyred for her faith at about the age of 14. In 1802 in the catacomb of Saint Priscilla on the Via Salaria in Rome the remains of a young woman were found. She was covered with stones that have ancient Christian symbols on them which indicated that the body was a martyr with the name Saint Philomena.

Her remains were exhumed and cataloged, stored and essentially forgotten about since there was virtually no information known of this young saints life. Then in 1805 Canon Francis de Lucia was inside the Treasury of Relics in the Vatican. When he came upon the relics of Saint Philomena, he was instantly overcome with a spiritual joy. He was so struck by this spiritual experience that he requested her relics be transferred to enshrine them in a chapel in Magnano.

Many miracles began to be experienced at the shrine, including cures of cancer, wounds that healed and a famous "Miracle of Magnano" where the venerable Pauline Jaricot was cured of a severe heart problem overnight. Philomena became the only person officially recognized as a saint solely on the basis of miraculous intercession and with virtually nothing absolutely known of her life.

Feast Day: August 11
Name Meaning: The loving song
Patron Saint of: Babies, bodily ills, children, children of Mary, infants, infertility, desperate causes, impossible causes.

St. Raphael the Archangel

S aint Raphael is one of the seven Archangels who stand before the throne of the Lord and one of the three angels mentioned by name in Holy Scripture. He is the leader of events in the Old Testament Book of Tobit.

He was sent by God to help Tobit, Tobiah and Sarah. At the time, Tobit was blind and Tobiah's betrothed, Sarah had seven bridegrooms die on the night of their weddings.

Raphael travelled with and guarded Tobiah into Mediah disguised as a man named Azariah.

Rafael helped him through his difficult times and guided him on how to safely enter into his marriage with Sarah. Tobiah credited Raphael with being able to have his wife and also he gave great joy to Sarah's parents for driving out the evil spirit in Sarah.

He also gave Raphael credit for his father seeing the light of heaven and for receiving all good things through his intercession.

Raphael's name means "God heals". This comes about because of the biblical story which states that he healed the earth when it was defiled by the sins of the fallen angels in the book of Enoch. He is also identified as the angel who moved the waters of the healing sheep pool in the Gospel of John.

Feast Day: October 24
Name Meaning: One heralded by God
Patron Saint of: Against nightmares, doctors, pharmacists, eye disease, physicians, happy meetings, mental illness, young people, travellers.

St. Raymond

Saint Raymond was born in Catalonia, in the year 1204, and was descended of a gentleman's family of small fortune.

He joined the new Order of Our Lady of Mercy for the redemption of captives, and was admitted to his profession at Barcelona by the holy founder, St. Peter Nolasco.

Within two or three years after his profession, he was sent into Barbary with a considerable sum of money, where he purchased, at Algiers, the freedom of a great number of slaves.

When all this treasure was exhausted, he gave himself up as a hostage for the ransom of certain others. This magnanimous sacrifice served only to anger the Muslims, who treated him with uncommon barbarity, until, fearing that if he died in their hands they would lose the ransom which was to be paid for the slaves for whom he remained a hostage, they gave orders that he should be treated with more humanity.

He was then permitted to go freely about the streets, which he took advantage of to comfort and encourage the Christians in their chains, and he converted and baptized some Muslims.

The governor, who was enraged, ordered our Saint to be barbarously tortured and imprisoned until his ransom was brought by some religious men of his Order, who were sent with it by St. Peter.

Upon his return to Spain, he was nominated cardinal by Pope Gregory IX, and the Pope, being desirous to have so holy a man about his person, called him to Rome. The Saint obeyed, but went no further than Cardona, when he was violently attacked, which proved fatal.

He died in the year 1240, at thirty years of age.

Feast Day: August 31
Name Meaning: The Mighty, Wise Protector
Patron Saint of: Child Birth, Expectant Mothers, Midwives, Infants.

St. Richard

Saint Richard was born in 1197 at Wyche, near Worcestershire, England. His father died when he was young and the family estate fell close to ruin. Richard took over the management of the property and restored it to good condition allowing him to pursue an education at Oxford. He continued his studies in Paris and then in Italy where he dedicated himself to the study of canon law and received his doctorate in law at Bologna.

He was elected Chancellor of the University of Oxford in 1235 and later chancellor to Edmund Rich,

Archbishop of Canterbury. St. Richard accompanied Edmund to the Cistercian Abbey of Pontigny, France after opposing the king about vacant sees.

Upon Edmund's death, Richard moved to the Dominican house at Orleans where he taught and studied theology and was finally ordained in 1243.

He returned to England where he was named chancellor to Boniface of Savoy, Edmund's successor. Upon the death of the Bishop of Chichester in 1244, Boniface recommended to the chapter to elect Richard; however, King Henry III opposed and refused Richard the temporalities of his see basically leaving him homeless. He relied on the charity of his clergy until he was finally allowed to take his duties as Bishop in 1246 when the Pope threatened to excommunicate Henry III. As Bishop, Richard gave away most of his money to the poor and compiled a number of statutes to bring discipline among the clergy concerning the regulation of the sacraments and church privileges. He lived a very simple, holy life. It is told that once, while saying Mass, he dropped the chalice and nothing spilled. The Pope appointed him to preach the crusade in London. While traveling to Dover to dedicate a new church to St. Edmund, Richard became sick. He died the morning after the consecration on April 3, 1253. He was canonized by Pope Urban IV in 1262.

Feast Day: April 3
Name Meaning: Powerful Rich Ruler
Patron Saint of: Coachmen.

St. Rita of Cascia

Saint Rita was born in Umbria, Italy, about the year 1386, and died at Cascia in the year 1456. Being the daughter of parents who were advanced in years, she met with much opposition when she let it be known of her intention of becoming a nun. Yielding to her parents desires, she married a cruel man. After converting him from his wicked ways, he was murdered by criminals.

Left alone in the world, she applied several times for admission into the Augustinian Convent at Cascia. Every application was refused, until God

Himself cleared away all obstacles and she entered the convent, made her profession and lived the life of a holy and devout religious for forty two years, "a shining example of every Christian virtue, pure as a lily, simple as a dove, and obedient as an angel." That "God is wonderful in His saints" is easily proven in the life of St. Rita. On one occasion Rita requested a rose to be brought to her from her garden at Porena in the middle of winter. The rose was found in full bloom. At another time she asked for a fig, and the same was found. The reports of these wonders spread far and wide, and people flocked to the convent from all parts of the world, only to receive in return for their faith in God through the prayers of Rita many spiritual and earthly favors. Because of the great number of miracles made possible by St. Rita, she is often called "The Saint of the impossible".

Feast Day: May 22
Name Meaning: The Pearl
Patron Saint of: Desperate Situations, Healing Wounds, Loneliness, Those suffering from tumors.

St. Robert Bellarmine

Saint Robert was born in Tuscany Italy in
October of the year 1542 AD. He was the
third child of ten in a family that was of
noble descent, yet they were a family without money.

His mother, a niece of Pope Marcellus II, was
dedicated to alms giving, prayer, meditation and fasting.
His father wanted Robert to enter into politics but
his boyhood education by the Jesuits and his mothers
holiness swayed his decision to enter the Society of
Jesus when he was 18 years old. He studied at many
Jesuit centers of learning over the next ten years and

was ordained in 1570 in Belgium. His first assignment was to be a professor of theology at the University of Louvain for six years. While there, he caught the attention of Pope Gregory XII who requested that Robert teach theology at the Collegio Romano in Rome. While he was there he wrote Disputationes de Controversiis Christianae Fidei Adversus Hujus Temporis Hereticos, the most complete work of the day to defend Catholicism against the attacks which Protestant kingdoms were spreading across Europe. This work helped stop the tide of false teachings and the forceful conversion of millions of the faithful by leaders who wanted the Churches power for themselves. He also wrote a childrens catechism and a teachers catechism. He later became rector of the College and then went on to become the provincial of the Jesuits in Naples and was also named a personal theologian to Pope Clement VIII. He wrote against King James I of England in defense of the Catholic Church because of the Kings split with the Church's authority. He was created a Cardinal in 1598 by the Pope and lived out the rest of his life in Rome where he gave most of his money to the poor. At one point he used his tapestries in his living quarters to clothe the poor, saying that "the walls won't catch cold."

He passed on in 1621 of natural causes and was canonized in 1930 by Pope Pius X.

Feast Day: September 17
Name Meaning: The one bright with fame
Patron Saint of: Canon lawyers, catechists, canonists.

St. Roch Confessor

The date of the birth of St. Roch can not be determined with exactness, but it is said that he was born about 1295, at Montpellier. His father held a position of power and influence in the city. After the death of his parents, when he was about twenty years of age, the young man had no inclination to take his father's position, but handed over the position to his uncle.

He then distributed his wealth to the poor and set out on a journey to Italy. At that time many people were afflicted with the plague, and the young man, dressed as a pilgrim, devoted his time, energy, and prayers to the care of those who had been stricken.

Wherever he went the plague disappeared before him, due to the fact that God gave him the power of working miracles on behalf of those who were suffering from the terrible disease. Having contracted the disorder himself, from which he recovered in the course of time, the young man went back to his own city in the year 1322. Not wishing to make himself known, he was cast into prison as a spy and died there five years later in the year 1327.

When his identity became known from some papers in his possession, he was given a public funeral, which was the occasion of numerous miracles. The relics of St. Roch are venerated at Venice, and the Church has established an arch-confraternity in his house.

His feast is celebrated on the 16th of August.

Feast Day: August 16
Name Meaning: The Rock
Patron Saint of: Skin Disease, Plague, Cholera, Invalids.

St. Rosalia

Rosalia was born in 1130 in Sicily. She was the daughter of Sinibald, Lord of Roses and Quisquina, a descendant of Charlemagne.

When she was young, she left home to live in a cave near Bivona so as to sacrifice her life to God. She later moved to a cave on Mount Pellegrino near Palermo. On the walls of the cave were found these words, "I, Rosalia, daughter of Sinibald, Lord of Roses and Quisquina, have taken the resolution to live in this cave for the love of my Lord, Jesus Christ."

She died in that cave in 1166.

A legend is told that in 1624, a terrible plaque broke out in Palermo. St. Rosalia appeared to a very sick woman and then to a hunter. She told the hunter to go to the cave and bring her bones to Palermo and have them carried in a procession through the streets. The hunter climbed to the cave and found the remains just as St. Rosalia had revealed to him. He arranged a procession to carry her relics through the city and three days later, the plaque ceased. A sanctuary was built in the cave where the hunter found her remains and every year on July 15 a celebration is held in Palermo called the festino. On her feast day, September 4, the tradition of walking barefoot from Palermo up to Mount Pellegrino honors St. Rosalia.

Rosalia is sometimes referred to as "The Little Saint" and is pictured as a young woman wearing a crown of roses and holding flowers or a book or a cross. She is known as the patron of Palermo, Sicily and El Hatillo, Venezuela.

Feast Day: September 4
Patron Saint of: Palermo, El Hatillo.

St. Rose of Lima

This lovely flower of sanctity, the first canonized Saint of the New World, was born at Lima in 1586.

She was christened Isabel, but the beauty of her infant face earned for her the title of Rose, which she then went by. At an early age she got a job to support her impoverished parents, and worked for them day and night. In spite of hardships, her beauty ripened with increasing age, and she was much and openly admired. For security she enrolled herself in the Third Order of St. Dominic, took St. Catherine of Siena as her model, and redoubled her penance. Her cell was a garden hut, her couch a box of broken tiles. Under her habit Rose wore a hair-shirt studded with iron nails, while, concealed by her veil, a silver crown armed with ninety points encircled her head.

More than once, when she thought of the prospect of a night of torture, a voice said, "My cross was yet more painful." The Blessed Sacrament seemed almost her only food.

Her love for it was intense. When the Dutch fleet prepared to attack the town, Rose took her place before the tabernacle, and wept that she was not worthy to die in its defense. All her suffering was offered for the conversion of sinners, and the thought of the multitudes in hell was always before her soul. She died A.D. 1617, at the age of thirty one.

Feast Day: August 20
Name Meaning: A Rose Flower
Patron Saint of: Florists, Gardeners, Needle Workers, Embroiderers.

St. Sebastian

*S*aint Sebastian was an officer in the Roman army, esteemed even by the pagans as a good soldier, and honored by the Church ever since as a champion of Jesus Christ.

Born at Narbonne, France, Sebastian came to Rome about the year 284, and entered the battle against the powers of evil. He found the twin brothers Marcus and Marcellinus in prison for the faith, and, when they were near giving up to the pleas of their relatives, to renounce Christ. He encouraged them to not give in to heretical teachings and to die for Christ.

God confirmed his words by a miracle, light shone around him while he spoke, he cured the sick by his prayers; and in his divine strength he led multitudes to the faith, among them the Prefect of Rome, with his son Tiburtius. He saw his disciples die before him, and one of them came back from Heaven to tell him that his own end was near. It was in a heated contest that St. Sebastian found the occasion of martyrdom.

He was betrayed by a false disciple, and was led before Diocletian, and at the emperor's command, pierced with arrows and left for dead.

But God raised him up again, and of his own accord he went before the emperor and summoned him to stop the persecution of the Church. Again sentenced, he was at last beaten to death by clubs, and crowned his works by the honor of a double martyrdom.

Feast Day: January 20
Name Meaning: The Venerable Revered One
Patron Saint of: Athletes, Archers, Soldiers.

St. Sophia

ophia was a widow living in Rome
during the reign of the Emperor Hadrian.
She had three daughters whom she named
after the virtues Faith, Hope and Love. Sophia was
a wise Christian who taught her daughters all about
the love of God. They lived a life of prayer, fasting
and almsgiving. They studied together the books
of the Prophets and the Apostles. They shared the
importance of spiritual reading, prayer and household
chores. Sophia instilled in her daughters the strength
and the wisdom of a life dedicated completely to God.

Because they did not hide their faith, word spread throughout Rome and the Emperor sent his servants to bring them to him. They understood the reason for his summons and immediately started to pray aloud for the strength to withstand any possible tortures.

Upon their arrival, Hadrian tried everything he could to get each of the young girls and their mother to deny Christ but none of his false promises swayed their faith. He sent them away for three days to live with a woman who tried also to turn them from God but Sophia just continued to teach her girls the truth each day. As they returned to Hadrian, one by one the girls were promised the riches of this world in exchange for their lives and each girl was brutally tortured in front of Sophia.

However, as her daughters prayed and sang of the glories of God, the beatings, the fire and the boiling oil seemed not to cause the girls any pain.

Each was finally killed by the sword after witnessing their faith to the crowd. Sophia buried her daughters together outside the city and after praying next to their grave for three days, she too died and was buried next to her three virtuous daughters.

Feast Day: September 17
Patron Saint of: Widows.

St. Stephen

 here is good reason to believe that St. Stephen was one of the seventy-two disciples of our blessed Lord.

Holy scripture calls him "A man full of faith and the Holy Spirit". He had the honor of being the first one to lay down his life for the faith of Christ.

After the Ascension he was chosen one of the seven original deacons.

The ministry of the seven was very fruitful; but Stephen especially, "full of grace and fortitude, did great wonders and signs among the people."

Many adversaries rose up to argue with him, but "they were not able to withstand the wisdom and spirit of which he spoke."

He was brought before the Sanhedrim, charged, like his Divine Master, with blasphemy against Moses and against God.

He boldly criticized the chief priests with their hard-hearted resistance to the Holy Spirit and with the murder of Jesus. They were stung with anger, and sentenced him to death. But when, "filled with the Holy Spirit and looking up to heaven, he cried out, 'Behold, I see the heavens opening and the Son of Man standing at the right hand of God,' they then rushed upon him, and dragged him throughout the city, and then stoned him to death.."

Feast Day: December 26
Name Meaning: The Crowned One
Patron Saint of: Bricklayers, Builders, Casket Makers, Deacons, Stoneworkers.

St. Teresa of Avila

aint Teresa was born in Spain in the year 1515. She grew up in a large family which was very religious. Her mother died when she was young and that had a great effect on her life.

She was in a convent school for two years and became a Carmelite nun soon thereafter. A few years into her profession she became ill and left for nearly two years. During this time she became a student of the practice of mental prayer. At about the age of 40 she had a second conversion and began to experience mystical prayer sometimes accompanied by visions and voices. A few years later she founded a convent and began to write books and started a reform movement returning to the primitive Carmelite rule.

This spread to the friars and her nuns around the world. She encountered great opposition from other clergy over her mysticism and her reforms but her persistence and strong character overcame them all.

As a writer Teresa is even more renowned than as a reformer. She wrote autobiographical and mystical works. Her books are still today cornerstones of spiritual reference. She is admired as a pioneer feminist and a literary figure who has made a great contribution to our knowledge of human psychology. Teresa died in Spain on October 4th 1582 and was canonized in 1628.

She was proclaimed a Doctor of the Church by Pope Paul VI in 1970.

Feast Day: October 15
Name Meaning: The reaper
Patron Saint of: People in need of grace, headaches, bodily ills, sick people, people in religious orders, loss of parents.

St. Therese of Lisieux

aint Therese of the Child Jesus and of the Holy Face was born in Alencon France on January 2nd 1873 and was baptized with the name Marie Francoise Therese.

She was the ninth and last child of her parents who had five daughters enter the religious life and four of them into the Carmelites.

Therese entered the Carmel at the age of fifteen and became a novice one year later and professed her vows the next year. For three years she had simple jobs to do and at seventeen she was put in charge of the sacristy.

During the nine years she spent in the convent she apparently never did anything remarkable in the outward sense but her writings were simply amazing.

She was told to write down all her childhood recollections and the resulting manuscript which covered all her life was published after her death as a book, The Story of a Soul.

The book took the Christian world by storm.

Sister Therese's "little way" of spiritual childhood, the way of trust and complete self-surrender, the way of simplicity and perfection in the doing of small things and daily duties, has become a pattern for millions of people. Graces without number are attributed to her intercession in Heaven and she is the saint of an era.

God enabled her to attain holiness through ordinary means in a short time. She was called to join the Lord in Heaven on September 30, 1887, she was not yet even twenty-five years old. She was declared a Doctor of the Church in 1997 by Pope John Paul II.

Feast Day: October 1
Name Meaning: Lovely woman
Patron Saint of: African missions, AIDS sufferers, bodily ills, tuberculosis.

St. Thomas Aquinas

Saint Thomas was born of noble parents at Aquino in Italy, A.D. 1226. When Thomas was five years old his father placed him under the care of the Benedictines of Monte Casino where he surpassed all his fellow students in intellect and virtue. At the age of seventeen, St. Thomas renounced the things of this world and chose to enter the Order of St. Dominic in spite of the opposition of his family. In 1243, at the age of nineteen, he joined the Dominicans of Naples. Some members of his family pressured him over a two year period to break his vows.

They even went so far as to send an impure woman to tempt him. But all their efforts were in vain and St. Thomas persevered in his vocation.

St. Thomas went to Cologne to study under Blessed Albert the Great, and after that to Paris, where for many years he taught philosophy and theology and became friendly with the king, St. Louis.

The Church has ever venerated his numerous writings as a treasure-house of sacred doctrine; while in naming him the Angelic Doctor she has indicated that his science is more divine than human.

The rarest gifts of intellect were combined in him with the tenderest piety. Prayer, he said, had taught him more than study.

Feast Day: January 28
Name Meaning: The Twin
Patron Saint of: Schools, Students, Publishers, Catholic Schools, Booksellers, Academics.

St. Veronica

Saint Veronica is believed to be the pious matron of Jerusalem who, moved with pity as Jesus carried the cross to Calvary, wiped His face with her handkerchief. The handkerchief or cloth was left with the clear and miraculous imprint of Jesus' face. In western tradition, Veronica was called to Rome by the Emperor Tiberius who was cured of his illness when she touched him with the cloth, which at her death she left to Pope Clement.

The story of Veronica found in the apocryphal Acts of Pilate identifies her as the woman mentioned in the Gospel of Matthew whom Jesus healed of a blood issue. In France, she was known as the wife of Zaccheus, who helped to evangelize the south of France when her husband became a hermit.

The veil was seen in Rome in the 8th century and by the request of Pope Boniface VIII placed in St. Peter's in 1297. In popular speech of the time, the veil was referred to as the Veronica, a name made up of the Latin word 'vera' and the Greek word 'icon', together meaning "true image".

It was mentioned in several medieval texts by the Bollandists, and Matthew of Westminister speaks of an image of Jesus called Veronica.

Thus, it is said that the name which referred to the cloth was mistaken for the name of a person. Although St. Veronica's name is not mentioned in Scripture and she is not included in Roman Martyrology, the memory of her single act of charity is commemorated in the 6th Station of the Cross and she is given a feast day. Veronica's veil, bearing the face of Christ and the Crown of Thorns is one of the most cherished relics of the Church.

Feast Day: July 12
Name Meaning: True image
Patron Saint of: Laundry workers, photographers.

St. Vincent de Paul

Saint Vincent was born in the year 1576 in a poor peasant family in France. He was very intelligent and as a young boy spent four years with the Franciscan friars getting an education.

He began his divinity studies at the University of Toulouse. He was ordained to the priesthood at the age of twenty. Soon after his ordination he was captured by Muslim slave traders and taken to Tunis. Vincent was able to convert one of his owners to Christianity and escape to France. Upon his return to France, he served as a parish priest near Paris where he instituted organizations to help the poor, nurse the sick and find jobs for the unemployed among many other deeds.

He was next appointed chaplain-general of the prisons of France. His tender charity brought hope into the galleys where only despair was found. He walked through the streets of Paris at night seeking the children who were abandoned to die.

Once robbers tried to accost him, thinking he had money with him, but when he opened his cloak they recognized him and knew of his deeds, so they fell at his feet for forgiveness. Not only was Vincent the savior of the poor but also of the rich, for he taught them to do works of mercy.

When the work for abandoned children was in danger of failing because of a shortage of funds, he assembled the ladies of the Association of Charity.

He told them to take care of the little children, as if they were their own. His work still continues today thru the St. Vincent DePaul Society, the Sisters of Charity and the Priests of the Mission.

St. Vincent died in the year 1660 and was canonized in 1737, by Pope Clement XII.

Feast Day: September 27
Name Meaning: The conquering one
Patron Saint of: Charities, charitable workers, hospitals, hospital workers, lepers, lost articles.

CONTENTS